RADIUM GIRLS

A Play in Two Acts
by
D.W. GREGORY

Dramatic Publishing
Woodstock, Illinois • England • Australia • New Zealand

"The best new play in New Jersey professional theatre."
The Star-Ledger

* * * *

IMPORTANT BILLING AND CREDIT REQUIREMENTS

AUTHOR'S NOTE

RADIUM GIRLS is a work of historical fiction. Although it is based on events that occurred in and around Orange, New Jersey, between 1918 and 1928, the characters and incidents portrayed have been shaped to serve the drama. Certain characters are entirely fictitious and others are based on multiple individuals.

PROGRAM CREDIT

RADIUM GIRLS was originally produced at Playwrights Theatre of New Jersey. Under a commission from Ensemble Studio Theatre of New York, it was subsequently revised. Any productions of this play **must** give program credit to these theatres, to read as follows:

"Originally produced by Playwrights Theatre of New Jersey and developed with a commissioning grant from The Ensemble Studio Theatre/Alfred P. Sloan Foundation Science & Technology Project."

This credit must appear in a type, manner or position of no less prominence than other producers of the play.

RADIUM GIRLS was first produced at Playwrights Theatre of New Jersey, May 11-28, 2000. Joseph Megel directed with the following cast:

Grace Fryer............................. Mary Bacon*
Arthur Roeder........................... Daren Kelly*
Kathryn Schaub/Societywoman/Board Member/
   Shopgirl/Mrs. Michaels................. Sarah Winkler*
Irene Rudolph/Miss Wiley/Harriet/Board Member/
   Miss Young/Scientist/Photographer....... Elizabeth Baron*
Sob Sister/Dr. Knef/Mrs. Roeder/MacNeil/
   Mrs. Fryer/Venecine Salesman............. T. Cat Ford*
Lee/Dr. Drinker/Bailey/Lovesick Cowboy/Flinn/
   Male Shopper/Roach .... Michael Perilstein*
Tom/Reporter/Berry/Board Member/Scientist...... Karl Kenzler*
Markley/Von Sochocky/Madame Curie/Widow/
   Martland/Store Owner..................... Jim Ligon*
Dialpainter/Second Reporter/Board Member/
   Assistant Stage Manager............... Jennifer Ginsberg
Production Stage Manager................ Uriel Menson*

*Actors Equity Association member

Casting by Michele Ortlip; set design by Jim Bazewicz; costumes by Valerie Holland Hughes, lighting by Ted Mather, sound by Dean Gray and Jonathan Taylor, makeup and properties by Tiffany M. Bazewicz. John Pietrowski, artistic director, Playwrights Theatre, Robert Carr, producer.

The play was also presented in a workshop production at Seton Hill University, Greensburg, Pa., in April 2001.

Under a grant from Ensemble Studio Theatre/Alfred P. Sloan Foundation Science & Technology Project, the play was subsequently revised. This revision was presented at the University of Washington-Seattle, March 6-17, 2002. Shanga Parker directed, with the following cast:

Grace Fryer . . . . Simone Fraser
Arthur Roeder . . . . Michael Koenen
Berry/Martland/Flinn/Store Owner . . . . Andy Kidd
Markley/Von Sochocky/Photographer . . . . Roni Weiss
Irene Rudolph/Wiley/Mrs. Michaels/
    Board Member #2 . . . . Kate Holte
Kathryn Schaub/Harriet/Societywoman/
    Board Member #1/Shopgirl . . . . Jessica Wells
Mrs. MacNeil/Mrs. Fryer/Sob Sister/Clerk/
    Elderly Widow . . . . Emily Cedergreen
Reporter/Tom Kreider/Dr. Knef. . . . . Michael Place
Mrs. Roeder/Madame Curie/Venecine Salesman/
    Board Member #3 . . . . Holly Patterson
Lee/Drinker/Bailey/Lovesick Cowboy/
    Male Shopper/Court . . . . Mathew Ahrens

Set by Matt Smucker, costumes by Ellen C. King, lights by Jesse Prince, sound by Matthew Jaeger. Stage manager, Audrey Murray.

The play was again revised and presented at Venture Theatre, Billings, Mont., Feb. 28-March 22, 2003. Mace Archer directed. In April 2003, the play was produced at the Catholic University of America, Grover Gardner directing.

NOTES ON PRODUCTION

RADIUM GIRLS is written to be performed by an ensemble of at least four men and five women, though a larger cast can perform it. The ensemble plays BOARD MEMBERS, members of the PUBLIC and various PRESS as the scenes require. All BOARD MEMBERS are men; all PRESS are men except SOB SISTER. Suggested doubling for major speaking parts:

With 9 actors:
ACTOR 1: GRACE
ACTOR 2: KATHRYN/BOARD MEMBER #1/
    SHOPGIRL/SOCIETYWOMAN/HARRIET
ACTOR 3: IRENE/MISS WILEY/BOARD MEMBER #2/
    PHOTOGRAPHER/MRS. MICHAELS
ACTOR 4: SOB SISTER/CLERK/ELDERLY WIDOW/
    MRS. FRYER/MACNEIL
ACTOR 5: MRS. ROEDER/MADAME CURIE/
    CUSTOMER/BOARD MEMBER #3
ACTOR 6: LEE/DRINKER/BAILEY/ FLINN/
    MALE SHOPPER/COURT/LOVESICK COWBOY
ACTOR 7: TOM/REPORTER/BERRY/KNEF
ACTOR 8: MARKLEY/ VON SOCHOCKY/
    STORE OWNER/VENECINE SALESMAN/MARTLAND
ACTOR 9: ROEDER

With 10 actors:
ACTOR 1: GRACE
ACTOR 2: KATHRYN/SOCIETYWOMAN/HARRIET/
    SHOPGIRL/BOARD MEMBER #1
ACTOR 3: IRENE/MISS WILEY/BOARD MEMBER #2/
    MRS. MICHAELS
ACTOR 4: SOB SISTER/MACNEIL/CLERK/MRS. FRYER
ACTOR 5: MRS. ROEDER/MADAME CURIE/
    CUSTOMER/BOARD MEMBER #3
ACTOR 6: LEE/BAILEY/DRINKER/LOVESICK
    COWBOY/MALE SHOPPER/COURT

ACTOR 7: BERRY/MARTLAND/FLINN/STORE OWNER
ACTOR 8: TOM/REPORTER/KNEF/VENECINE SALESMAN
ACTOR 9: MARKLEY/VON SOCHOCKY/ELDERLY
   WIDOW/PHOTOGRAPHER
ACTOR 10: ROEDER

The action takes place in a variety of places in and around Orange, N.J., between 1918 and 1928. The style is meant to be cinematic, briskly paced and mixing naturalistic scenes with more comic, presentational scenes. Of necessity, set and furnishings must be simple: eight wooden chairs and two or three narrow tables, which remain at all times. Such a set should accommodate fluid transitions from scene to scene; in fact, certain scenes are meant to be transitional—taking place while the set is changed. A sense of place is created by the rearrangement of the tables and chairs, with the help of lights, sound, props, and costumes, to suggest different locations—home, factory, office, hospital, etc. All set changes are to be effected by the actors in view of the audience, and props should be minimal. Costume changes, too, must be simple—only what is needed to present a transformation to new characters.

NOTE ON PRONUNCIATON

As a few of the names have confounded some actors in various productions, I here offer suggested pronunciations:

Roeder – REED-er
Von Sochocky – VON Sa-SHOCK-y
Schaub – SHAWB
Amelia Maggia – a-MAL-ia MAD-ja
Albina – al-BUY-na
Quinta – KIN-ta
Venecine – VEH-nah-seen
Radithor – RAY-da-thor
Knef – NEF
Kreider – CRY-der

RADIUM GIRLS

A Play in Two Acts
For at least 4 men and 5 women, extras

CHARACTERS

THE WOMEN IN THE FACTORY

GRACE FRYER . . . . A top-notch dialpainter,
15 at the start of the play, 26 at its close.

KATHRYN SCHAUB . . . . Her friend, another dialpainter,
also 15 at the start of the play.

IRENE RUDOLPH . . . . Kathryn's cousin,
17 at the start of the play. Later she is in her 20s.

MRS. ALMA MACNEIL . . . . Their supervisor.

THE COMPANY MEN

ARTHUR ROEDER . . . . . President of the U.S. Radium Corp.,
34 at start of the play, 65 at its close.

EDWARD MARKLEY . . . . Counsel for the company.

C.B. "CHARLIE" LEE . . . . Vice president,
later president of the company.

DR. VON SOCHOCKY . . . . . . Founder of U.S. Radium Corp.,
inventor of the luminous paint.

THEIR FAMILY and FRIENDS

TOM KREIDER . . . . Grace's boyfriend,
several years older than she.

DIANE ROEDER. . . . . Married to Arthur Roeder.

HARRIET ROEDER. . . . . Their daughter.
Nine years old at first, later she is in her 30s.

ANNA FRYER . . . . Grace's mother.

THE ADVOCATES
KATHERINE WILEY . . . . The executive director,
                                New Jersey Consumer's League.
RAYMOND BERRY . . . . An attorney for the dialpainters.

THE SCIENTISTS
DR. CECIL DRINKER . . . . A Harvard industrial hygienist.
DR. HARRISON MARTLAND . The county medical examiner.
DR. JOSEPH KNEF . . . . A dentist.
DR. MARIE CURIE. . . . . Discovered radium.
FREDERICK FLINN, Ph.D. . . . . Columbia University
                                industrial hygienist.

THE PRESS
REPORTER (JACK YOUNGWOOD) . . . . A reporter,
                                Newark Ledger.
SOB SISTER (NANCY JANE HARLAN) . . A tabloid reporter,
                                New York Graphic.

THE WITNESSES
WILLIAM J.A. BAILEY . . . . An entrepreneur, manufacturer of
                                Radithor.
MRS. MICHAELS . . . . A consumer of Radithor.
SOCIETY WOMAN . . . . Mrs. James (Cora) Middleton,
                                a well-bred woman.
CLERK . . . . An overworked public employee.

OTHER MEMBERS OF THE PUBLIC WHO TAKE AN
INTEREST IN THE CASE.

THE TIME: The 1920s.
THE PLACE: Orange, New Jersey.

ACT ONE

SCENE 1

AT RISE: *A room in the U.S. Radium plant. GRACE alone in a pin spot. GRACE is speaking as if she is in the office of her attorney, RAYMOND BERRY, who is either unseen or in shadow.*

GRACE. So much light. *(She looks around, taking in the memory of the dialpainting studio.)* Daylight. All the time. And on sunny days—you almost felt like you were sitting outside. It was that bright.

BERRY'S VOICE. That surprised you, Grace?

GRACE. It was a factory. I thought it would be dark. And dirty.

BERRY. Then why go to work there?

GRACE. I was fifteen. It was time I paid my own way.

BERRY. Pay your own way? What about school?

GRACE. Oh, I didn't miss it so much. The girls were all so nice and the work wasn't hard. It wasn't like factory work, really. It was more like art, painting those dials. We were artists.

(Crossfade to ROEDER, opposite, speaking as if he is in his own office, where the company lawyer, EDWARD MARKLEY, is questioning him. Like BERRY, MARKLEY is either unseen or in shadow.)

11

ROEDER. I'm not really the one you should be talking to. Von Sochocky. He's the one you should talk to.

MARKLEY'S VOICE. Now, Arthur. You know he won't talk to us.

ROEDER. It was his process.

(Behind him, lights rise slowly on the room in the factory, where IRENE and KATHRYN, two dialpainters, are mixing up paint.)

MARKLEY'S VOICE. Tell me about that process, Arthur. You used a powder…

ROEDER. We used a powder. The girls mixed it with an adhesive to make the paint. And that business with the brushes—I didn't invent that. They were doing that when I started there.

MARKLEY. But you knew about it.

ROEDER. We all knew about it. We just didn't realize what it meant.

(As lights fade on ROEDER, they rise full on IRENE and KATHRYN, giggling and applying paint to their faces. Enter GRACE.)

GRACE. Irene?

IRENE. In here!

GRACE. Irene? What are you doing?

IRENE. Shut the door.

KATHRYN. Amelia's workin' inspection today.

GRACE. Is that bad?

IRENE. Not for us.

KATHRYN. She's gonna be sittin' in this room all day. By herself, in the dark, checkin' dials.

IRENE. Poor thing.

KATHRYN. Poor thing.

IRENE. So we're gonna give her a little surprise.

KATHRYN. Boo! Like the Cheshire Cat! *(IRENE and KATHRYN laugh.)*

GRACE. Oooh! Won't that make her mad?

KATHRYN. Let her get mad.

IRENE. That's half the fun.

GRACE. I don't want to make her mad.

IRENE. Oh, Grace! Do you have to be that way about everything?

GRACE. What way?

KATHRYN. Your teeth, Grace. Put some on your teeth. *(GRACE consents to be painted.)*

IRENE. Ain't like Amelia don't deserve it. She paints more dials than any girl on the floor. And can't be bothered to talk to nobody either. You say "Amelia! What's new?" She just looks at ya funny.

GRACE. I don't think she can speak much English

IRENE. It wouldn't kill her to smile, would it? *(Footsteps and voices off.)*

KATHRYN. She's comin'.

IRENE. Get the light!

(KATHRYN turns out the light, and they crouch down giggling as someone enters the room. Then they jump up, their faces glowing like jack-o'-lanterns in the dark. A scream, laughter, and the lights go up again, revealing a stunned MRS. MACNEIL, ROEDER and VON SOCHOCKY. If this effect cannot be achieved, then

MACNEIL and others can walk in on them before KATHRYN gets to the light. In that case the beat continues, if necessary, as follows:

[KATHRYN. Where's the switch?
IRENE *(going for the switch)*. For pity's sakes, Kathryn!])

(Enter ROEDER, VON SOCHOCKY and MACNEIL.)

IRENE. Oops.

GRACE. Mrs. MacNeil!

MACNEIL. Paintin' yer faces. Have ya gone off yer minds?

IRENE. It was just a joke.

MACNEIL. Just a joke? A joke like that can lose a girl her job.

VON SOCHOCKY. Now, now, Mrs. MacNeil. I'm sure that's not necessary.

MACNEIL. I don't tolerate no foolishness, Doctor.

VON SOCHOCKY. Ja, very good. Foolishness, we don't want. Do we? Mr. Roeder. This is the inspection room. All the dials come here that are painted. And here, are some of the girls who should on the floor be working. Girls, this is Mr. Roeder. My new vice president. And your new plant manager.

MACNEIL. And I was just telling Mr. Roeder what a fine bunch of girls we have here. I'm sure now he must think I'm halfway out of my mind.

VON SOCHOCKY. Mr. Roeder. Perhaps you have some words for the girls? Mrs. MacNeil? *(He ushers MRS. MACNEIL out of the room.)*

ROEDER. Well. *(A moment as he regards them.)* Girls. This paint you've been playing with. It's very expensive. You realize this? *(Mumbled acknowledgment.)* It takes several tons of ore to produce a single gram of radium. That's a lot of work—hard work, for the men in the extraction plant. But they do this work gladly. You understand why? Why they work so hard? What we are all working for?

GRACE. The war?

ROEDER. That's right. The war. The dials you paint save lives, girls. Our boys in the field depend on them. To read them in the dark, no mistaking what they see. Otherwise…some of those boys won't be coming home. So, girls. If you play around and don't take the work seriously…well, you're playing into the hands of the Kaiser. And we don't want that, do we?

GIRLS. No sir… Oh, no! Etc.

ROEDER. So let's get back to work now and leave the tomfoolery to home. *(The GIRLS file away, but GRACE lingers.)*

GRACE. Mr. Roeder? I just—I just wanted to say. I—I am sorry. I won't do nothin' like this ever again.

ROEDER. Well, dear. Just keep this in mind: If you do right by us, we'll do right by you.

(A tableau, then:)

SCENE 2

(Enter SOB SISTER and REPORTER as GRACE and ROEDER break.)

SOB SISTER. May 17, 1921. Nancy Jane Harlan here—for the New York Graphic! The New York Graphic's only girl reporter!

REPORTER. Jack Youngwood for the Newark Ledger! Newark's first source for news!

(The scene transforms to a street scene of excitement with band music, carnival atmosphere. ROEDER and GRACE join CROWD.)

SOB SISTER. Madame Marie Curie, eminent French scientist, embarks on a whistle-stop tour of the United States.

REPORTER. First stop—New York City, where she is greeted by an enthusiastic crowd of well-wishers!

SOB SISTER. The high priestess of science is headed for Washington to receive a gift of one gram of radium—valued at one hundred thousand dollars!

REPORTER. Purchased for her by the members of the Marie Curie Radium Club—an association of one hundred thousand American women—

SOB SISTER. —who each gave one dollar to support humanitarian research with radium.

IRENE. Grace! Over here!

GRACE. Irene! Look! I got my certificate. Member, Marie Curie Radium Club!

IRENE. You gave a dollar?

GRACE It's all for science!

IRENE. Science! What about my room and board?

GRACE. Oooh! There she is!

(MADAME CURIE steps up to the podium with VON SOCHOCKY and SOCIETYWOMAN. This is Cora Middleton, a well-heeled, well-spoken woman of dignity. She takes a great interest in science—and any other issue likely to place her at the center of excitement.)

SOCIETYWOMAN. Welcome all, welcome all! I must ask you, ladies and gentlemen of the press, please limit your questions! Madame Curie is about to embark on an exhaustive tour of the country. And she is under strict doctor's orders to rest—although, in the typical fashion of a scientist who can think only of her research, her life's work—she has refused to rest! *(Approval from the CROWD.)*

REPORTER. Madame Curie! What will you do with the radium?

MADAME CURIE *(in a thick Polish accent)*. Eh?

REPORTER. What will you do with the radium?

MADAME CURIE. Uh…I will continue my experiments to find better methods for ze treatment of ze cancer. *(Applause.)*

SOB SISTER. Is radium a cure for all cancer?

MADAME CURIE. Cure for ze cancer? Yes, yes. Cure for ze cancer! Zat is so. It has already cured all kinds of ze cancer.

SOB SISTER. But some doctors dispute that!

MADAME CURIE. Zen zey do not understand ze method. Zere is no question—radium will cure ze cancer.

SOB SISTER. Madame Curie!

REPORTER. Madame Curie!

SOB SISTER. Madame Curie! How have you managed to devote yourself both to science—and to your children?

MADAME CURIE. Ah. It has not been easy. *(Laughter from CROWD.)* But my daughters share my gratitude to ze American women for zere interest in science and my work. I am most grateful.

REPORTER. Madame Curie!

SOB SISTER. Madame Curie!

REPORTER. Madame Curie!

SOCIETYWOMAN. No more questions! Madame Curie is on a tight schedule! Mrs. Andrew Carnegie has sent a car—and will escort Dr. Curie personally—as will I—to Washington—where President Harding will present the gift—of one gram of radium! *(Cheers and excitement as MADAME CURIE and CROWD exits leaving ROEDER and LEE.)*

ROEDER. You see that, Charlie? That is a marketing opportunity! Let's send her one of our customer's watches. Courtesy, the United States Radium Corporation!

LEE. We'll need a press release. *(LEE takes notes as ROEDER ruminates.)*

ROEDER. Radium isn't just for scientists to study. The average American can share in its glory every night. Luminous watches, luminous clocks! Anyone who thinks these are just novelties, consider all the other advances that have taken place in the past fifty years—the electric light. The telegraph—

LEE. The telephone!

ROEDER. The automobile! Inventions all once dismissed as novelties—as toys—

LEE. —are now essentials to modern life. Got it. That ought to sell some watches.

ROEDER. Watches, absolutely. But that's not where the growth is now, Charlie. You heard the lady, it's the medical market.

LEE. And Standard Chemical owns it.

ROEDER. Only because Von Sochocky lets them take it. But if we wanted to, we could get half their business. It's just a matter of positioning.

LEE. Standard Chemical publishes its own journal. Sends it out monthly—to twelve thousand doctors. We could do something similar.

ROEDER. Something scholarly. That the doctors would respect.

LEE. A bibliography. Listing every article ever published on radium...

ROEDER. But with capsule reports—to save the doctors time. They'd get the information, find it fast

LEE. And have us to thank for it.

ROEDER. We'll send it to every doctor in the U.S. Radium Society.

LEE. Every doctor in the American Medical Association.

ROEDER. That's the spirit, Charlie. Advertising. That's the wave of the future. It's not just the product—it's the way you promote it.

(ROEDER and LEE exit as factory whistle blows.)

SCENE 3

(The studio. The GIRLS enter to set up for work. It is four years after the first scene; they are older, more settled, and a large diamond engagement ring twinkles on GRACE's finger.)

KATHRYN. You shoulda seen it, Grace! The church was filled with flowers. Lilies and carnations and orchids. You know how Amelia loved orchids.

IRENE. They weren't orchids.

KATHRYN. They were orchids, Irene.

IRENE. Flags.

KATHRYN. Orchids. I know an orchid when I see one. Purple orchids. Oh, and that smell. Grace—that smell. What was that smell, it was like, like—

GRACE. Flowers?

KATHRYN. No. It was like—heaven. I was gonna say, it was like heaven.

IRENE. Like heaven? Kathryn: It was just a funeral. Ya make it out like it was some Valentino picture.

KATHRYN. It wasn't just a funeral. It was Amelia's. And it was beautiful. Ya shoulda seen it. The church was like...the botanical gardens...and the company sent a big spray of flowers, too. Carnations.

IRENE. Mums.

KATHRYN. Yellow carnations.

IRENE. Those were mums.

GRACE. Well it sounds like a nice service anyhow.

(Enter MACNEIL.)

MACNEIL. Girls, girls! The whistle's already gone. Now, then. I've received new instructions this day. We're going back to the old way of pointin' the brushes. We was losin' too much paint in the cloth. *(She collects the cloth. As she does the GIRLS point the brush on their lips. GRACE hesitates.)*

GRACE. But—

MACNEIL. Yes, Grace? Something ya wish to say?

GRACE. Dr. Von Sochocky told me not to do that. He said it's—unsanitary.

MACNEIL. Unsanitary? Well, I can't hardly believe he'd say such a thing. We've done this as long as I've been here. Ya must've misunderstood him.

GRACE. Yes ma'am. *(GRACE surrenders the cloth and tips the brush on her lips.)*

MACNEIL. And you're not to get new brushes until you've done with the old. And they got to be so bad they can't get a point no more.

KATHRYN *(to IRENE).* Ya can't make quota like that!

MACNEIL. Well, you'll do your best, then. Since I have my instructions.

IRENE. I need a new brush. *(MRS. MACNEIL looks at the brush, then gives IRENE another.)*

MACNEIL. It's not for us to be askin' questions, is it? It's for us to do the work. *(MACNEIL moves away, and the GIRLS set to painting, pointing the brushes on their lips as they proceed.)*

KATHRYN. I have my instructions, girls, I have my instructions.

IRENE. Here's an instruction for you, MacNeil: Let some of the starch outta yer corset. *(KATHRYN laughs.)*

GRACE. Was she at the service?

IRENE. MacNeil? Are you kidding? Y'think she'd cross the street for her own mother?

KATHRYN. Most everybody else was, though. You was about the only girl from the floor who wasn't there.

GRACE. I wanted to come. But Ma was workin' and I had to watch the little'uns.

KATHRYN. Ya coulda brought 'em.

GRACE. All seven?

KATHRYN. Well if it was me, I'da tried to get there.

IRENE. Just lay off. Grace feels bad as it is.

GRACE. Were many of the fellas there?

KATHRYN. Oh yeah—lots of fellas from downstairs. Mr. Roth from the front office. Dr. Von Sochocky was there. And Mr. Roeder.

IRENE. And he left early.

KATHRYN. So? He was there all the same. Oh! And, Grace—you know that fella from crystalizing, what's his name, the one with the red hair? He was there. Y'know who I mean?

GRACE. Oh! The tall fella with the freckles?

KATHRYN. That's the one—who snaps his fingers all the time.

GRACE. George!

IRENE. Jerry.

KATHRYN. I think it is George.

IRENE. It's Jerry. Jerry Mallon. He's the one who was always talkin' to Amelia in the day room.

KATHRYN. That's right! Ooh, Grace! When the mass was over, he goes over to the coffin— And he goes like this, like this he goes— *(She puts her hand to her lips and slowly blows a kiss to an imaginary coffin.)*

GRACE. No!

KATHRYN. Yes!

GRACE. Really?

KATHRYN. Really! *(They both squeal excitedly.)*

IRENE. Oh for pity's sakes.

KATHRYN. Well, he did. Nobody could believe it.

IRENE. So what if he did?

KATHRYN. So what? He was in love with her, that's so
what. Don't you think so, Grace?

GRACE. Well I guess he had to be. If he did that.

KATHRYN. And can you imagine? Can you imagine? If
he loved her and he never told her, never could bring
himself to say! Because...because she was *so* beautiful...and...and he was *so* shy. And now it's too late. It's
too late, their love is forever thwarted. He didn't tell her,
and he'll never get a chance ever again. *(They reflect on
this realization somberly.)*

GRACE. Poor Amelia.

KATHRYN. Poor Amelia!

IRENE. Poor kid.

KATHRYN. Her family took it awful bad, Grace. Albina,
Quinta, everybody. Everyone of 'em cryin'. Even her father, cryin' so bad. I never saw a man cry before and not
like that—just bawlin' like a baby.

IRENE. And y'know why, too.

GRACE. 'Cause their daughter had died.

IRENE. What she died *from.*

KATHRYN. Irene. Don't go spreadin' stories.

IRENE. It's not a story. Albina told us. No reason Grace
shouldn't know.

GRACE. Know what? Know what? *(KATHRYN whispers
something awful.)* Amelia?

KATHRYN. Ain't it awful? Albina said her father's fit to
be tied, too—six girls at home and ain't none of 'em
ever goin' to a dance again.

IRENE. All because Amelia upped and died from *syphilis!*

GRACE. Sh!

IRENE. I can't help it if that's what she died from!

GRACE. You don't know that for sure.

KATHRYN. It's on the death certificate.

IRENE. Anemia and complications from syphilis!

GRACE. But Amelia was ever so nice.

IRENE. Guess she got around more than we knew.

GRACE. Maybe it's a mistake. Maybe the doctor got it wrong.

IRENE. Come on.

GRACE. He coulda got it wrong. Doctors are wrong sometimes.

KATHRYN. That's true. Doctor was wrong about Aunt Ivy.

IRENE. What's Mama got to do with it?

KATHRYN. Irene, don't you remember? Up to the day she died, doctor said Aunt Ivy would be fine. Said take a cup a tea, get a good night's rest. And two days later we was taking her to Rosedale cemetery.

(Enter MACNEIL, ROEDER, VON SOCHOCKY, carrying his coat and a small, leather-bound book.)

MACNEIL. Girls, girls! Your attention, please. The gentlemen are here to make an announcement.

ROEDER. Thank you, Mrs. MacNeil. Girls, we are here to put a few rumors to rest.

VON SOCHOCKY. —and to explain some changes, ja?

ROEDER. Yes. As some of you may have heard by now, Dr. Von Sochocky is stepping down—and he wanted to take this opportunity—

VON SOCHOCKY *(cutting him off)*. ...to make with goodbye. And Mr. Roeder has kindly consented. *(He pauses, looking for the words.)* Some of you I have known since you were little girls. Coming here during the war. Working so hard! Day after day at the bench, two hundred, three hundred, some of you, five hundred dials a day! So excited to be part of our work here. When this company I start, in my own kitchen, mixing up the paint, I knew I found something miraculous, to make life better…easier… And now…what do I read?… *(He taps the red book thoughtfully.)* …more and more uses are there for the radium… More than I dreamed possible. *(He stops. MRS. MACNEIL dabs her eyes with a kerchief.)*

MACNEIL. Thank you, Doctor.

ROEDER *(embarrassed by the emotion)*. Yes, thank you, Doctor. *(Brightening.)* Now, girls. The doctor is a busy man and must be on his way. So let's wish him the best of luck in his new business ventures! *(Applause from GIRLS.)* Very good, then, girls—

VON SOCHOCKY. And Mr. Roeder. Let us good luck wish to you also. To the plate he steps as your new company president! Our congratulations to you.

ROEDER. Thank you.

VON SOCHOCKY. When Mr. Roeder came four years ago to us, I saw in him a young man of great enterprise—

ROEDER. Thank you—

VON SOCHOCKY *(overlapping)*. And great ambition!

ROEDER. Yes, thank—

VON SOCHOCKY *(overlapping—a false cheerfulness)*. Little did I guess the direction your ambition would take. But! One of the things that makes this country great is the opportunity it presents to a young man…and his friends.

ROEDER. And so, girls—

VON SOCHOCKY. And so, ladies! Let us wish Mr. Roeder the very best in the new direction he intends the company to take.

IRENE *(to KATHRYN)*. New direction?

VON SOCHOCKY. With the slowdown in dialpainting—

ROEDER *(overlapping)*. Now, Doctor—

VON SOCHOCKY *(overlapping)*. And business moving into the medical market, there's going to be lots of changes, ja? *(A moment.)*

ROEDER. What the doctor is referring to...some of our larger customers are setting up their own dialpainting studios.

VON SOCHOCKY. Which means less work for our girls here.

ROEDER. In the short run. Things may be slower here. However, the Waterbury Clock Company in Connecticut will need help setting up its new studio. We were intending to make an announcement next week. We'll make it now. Mrs. MacNeil?

MACNEIL. Uh. Well. We'll be askin' some of you girls to go on up there.

ROEDER. The work is supervisory in nature. Which means more pay. You have some girls in mind?

MACNEIL. Louise Conlon was one. Sarah Deutsch. Lena McCarthy...and Kathryn Schaub. *(Reaction from GIRLS.)* I have the entire list downstairs. I'll post it today?

ROEDER. Fine. There you have it, girls. As we are all on the clock...we'll leave you to your work.

VON SOCHOCKY. Thank you, ladies. My best wishes to you.

MACNEIL. That's back to work with you, girls. *(Exit MACNEIL, VON SOCHOCKY, ROEDER.)*

GRACE. You gonna do it, Kathryn? You gonna take that job?

KATHRYN *(overlapping).* Would you, Grace? Would you go to Connecticut? *(IRENE feels dizzy.)*

GRACE. Oh, I don't know. That's awful far from home. Tommy would have a fit!

KATHRYN. Oh come on, Grace, it'd be fun! Won't it be fun, Irene! Irene? *(IRENE sits with her head in her hands.)*

GRACE. Irene? Honey, you all right?

IRENE. Huh? Yeah, sure. Why wouldn't I be all right? *(A beat as GRACE studies her.)* What?

GRACE *(quietly).* Your mouth is bleeding.

(IRENE wipes her mouth with her hand. She studies the blood on her hand as if she had never seen blood before. Tableau—then break. Cross to:)

SCENE 4

(The dining room of Grace's childhood home. TOM is eating leftovers as MRS. FRYER clears the table.)

MRS. FRYER. Thirty-five dollars a week and she quits the place.

TOM. More to life than money.

MRS. FRYER. That's what ya say when you're young, Tom. But you'n Grace get to be my age—with a house fulla yer kids underfoot. You'll thank God for every penny ya put by.

TOM. We got money put by.

MRS. FRYER. How much?

TOM. Enough to get married on.

MRS. FRYER. Don't take much to *get* married on. Do ya have enough to *stay* married on?

TOM. You let us get married, we'll find out.

(TOM laughs as GRACE enters.)

GRACE. Are you still eatin', Tommy?

TOM. It's good.

GRACE *(takes the plate)*. You're going to get fat.

MRS. FRYER *(takes the plate back)*. Gotta keep up his strength. He works hard for his money.

GRACE. Don't start, Ma.

MRS. FRYER. I didn't say nothin'. It's your father who hit the roof over it.

GRACE. He didn't hit the roof.

MRS. FRYER. You shoulda seen the man's face, Tom, when he found out Grace wasn't workin' no more. Most girls would give their eyeteeth for a job like that—good money, easy work, nice-lookin' fellas around the plant—

TOM. You didn't tell me about them, Grace.

GRACE. Wasn't that many of 'em. Hardly seemed worth the mention.

MRS. FRYER. And she leaves it all behind. For reasons unknown. I'm tired of it up there, she says. Are you tired of the paycheck, I says? Who needs a paycheck, she says. I got me a boyfriend to take me out Saturdays.

TOM. She said that?

GRACE. Oh you know I didn't. And for your information I got a job. I start at the bank on Monday.

MRS. FRYER. Oh yeah, the bank! And what's it pay?

GRACE. Enough.

MRS. FRYER. Enough. Always enough. You know what that means, Tom. It don't come close to what it pays up at the radium plant.

GRACE. It's office work.

MRS. FRYER. Office work! Well, I guess that means you'll be spendin' more money on clothes, then. *(She takes TOM's empty plate and leaves.)*

TOM. Boy, she is really steamed at you.

GRACE. I don't see what difference it makes so long as I'm workin' somewheres.

TOM. Don't make no difference to me. I just thought ya liked it up there. *(He looks at her.)*

GRACE *(avoiding his gaze)*. Sure I liked it. I worked there four years.

TOM. So? I been deliverin' mail almost eight years. I plan to keep on deliverin' mail another twenty or thirty years. *(Tapping on the table.)* If I'm lucky. Nothin' like steady work and a good pension to help ya sleep at night.

GRACE. I don't have a pension, and I sleep just fine.

TOM. I bet you do. *(She swats at him and he grabs her.)*

TOM. So how come ya quit, Grace?

GRACE. Lots of girls are quittin'. Work is slow. Besides, since Irene left, it's just not as much fun. And wouldn't ya rather have a girlfriend who works in a bank?

TOM. Not as much as I'd like to have a wife who don't work anywhere.

GRACE. Close yer eyes. I gotta surprise for ya.

TOM *(hoping for a kiss)*. Yeah? Want for me to pull the shades?

GRACE. Not that kinda surprise. Close yer eyes. *(She retrieves two pieces of paper and puts them in front of him.)* Now look.

TOM. Wallpaper.

GRACE. For the baby's room.

TOM. Baby's room! Ya won't kiss me and you're talkin' about babies?

GRACE. There's gonna be babies eventually, Tommy.

TOM. Well, sure. But y'know, Grace, most girls—they get married before they decorate the nursery.

GRACE. Plan ahead for once. Pick one.

TOM. They're both the same.

GRACE. No they're not. This one has big flowers, and that one has little flowers. So pick one.

TOM. This some kinda test?

GRACE. No. It's just wallpaper.

TOM. It is some kinda test.

GRACE. Pick one, Tommy.

TOM. That one.

GRACE. Really?

TOM. The other one then.

GRACE. Which do you like, though?

TOM. They're both nice.

GRACE. This one is pretty, don't you think?

TOM. That one, then.

GRACE. But I want you to like it, too.

TOM. If you like it, I'll like it. Wallpaper is wallpaper.

GRACE. No it isn't. Ya gotta pick somethin' ya can stand to look at for twenty years.

TOM. Same way ya pick women?

GRACE. Keep it up, smarty pants. You won't never get that kiss.

TOM. Okay, this one. This one, hands down.

GRACE. I like it, too. A nice neutral yellow goes with either a boy or a girl. And until the baby comes, ya can use the room for other things.

TOM. Yeah? Like what?

GRACE. Like... A painting studio, maybe?

TOM. A painting studio maybe? Didn't you get enough of painting at work?

GRACE. Not the kind I wanted to do. Tommy. I used to paint watercolors at school...and ever since I went to work, I don't have no time. What with watchin' the kids, and helpin' Ma... Once we get married, I just want some time...just a little time to myself. So's I can do watercolors. Or oils maybe. Maybe portraits, in oil. I could paint yer picture if ya like.

TOM. Why not? Paint a big picture of me and we'll hang it in the outhouse. All our friends will come round just to use the can, so's they can look at it.

GRACE. Oh, the way you talk sometimes!

TOM. Aw, Grace. Ya wanna paint pictures. Paint pictures. I ain't gonna stop ya.

GRACE. You say that now, Tommy. But once we're married—you'll change your tune.

TOM. Sure. I'll be whistling Dixie.

GRACE. Wait'll you come home some night all wore out. Some Christmas maybe, when every customer on yer route's had three times the mail. And maybe some dog took after ya. And some old lady kept ya waitin' on her stoop, tellin' ya all about her grandchildren. And you wouldn't have the heart to tell her ya can't talk— I know you. So ya come home, all cranky and late besides. Hungry—wantin' yer dinner. And there I am, with my easel set up in the kitchen, and a drop cloth on the floor, my paints all over the table. And yer dinner nowhere in sight. What would ya say then?

TOM. Better be a picture of me yer paintin'.

GRACE. I know what ya'd say. Where's my dinner? That's what ya'd say! Where's my dinner.

TOM. Well, sure. But I'd still admire the paintin'. Just want to look at it on a full stomach is all. *(He gets his arms around her.)*

TOM. So how'd I do? Pick the right wallpaper?

GRACE. I don't know. Maybe I'll go look at stripes.

TOM. Stripes! Polka dots! I don't care! Let's just get married, Grace! Yer plenty old enough! Tell yer Ma we ain't waitin' no more—we'll just run off!

GRACE. Tommy! We are not runnin' off. We're gonna do it right! A nice church weddin' with flowers and music. And then a week at the seashore. Just us! And after that, we get set up in our own place. You'll see. It'll be worth the wait. *(He gets a kiss.)*

TOM. Yer mouth hurt ya?

GRACE. Yeah. The dentist wants to pull another tooth. In the back.

TOM. Well. What's a tooth?

(He kisses her cheek. Cross to:)

SCENE 5

(Roeder's office. MARKLEY, ROEDER and LEE. MARKLEY is reading a letter.)

MARKLEY. Hazel Kuser. Any connection to the others?

LEE. Only by virtue of employment.

ROEDER. Except she's got a good lawyer.

LEE. Knows how to write a good letter anyway, that lawyer.

MARKLEY. And she no longer works here?

LEE. Left six months ago.

ROEDER. This makes four now.

LEE. Three.

ROEDER. Four if you count the Maggia girl.

LEE. I wouldn't include her.

ROEDER. She worked here.

LEE. She also worked other places. And what she died from—you couldn't pick up here. At least, I don't think you can.

ROEDER. That's not funny, Charlie. Besides, that's just idle talk.

LEE. In my experience, there's usually something to the idle talk. When it comes to girls like that.

MARKLEY. From a large family, wasn't she?

LEE. Italians. The conditions they live in! Ten, twelve people in three rooms. It's a wonder they don't all die of one infection or another.

MARKLEY. Three, then. And how many dead?

ROEDER. Only Miss Maggia. But I haven't heard from her people.

MARKLEY. It's too late for them anyway. The statute of limitations is two years. But Miss Kuser is another story. She's in a position to make some trouble now.

ROEDER. In all the time I've been here. No one has so much as slipped on the floor. And now this.

LEE. We're talking about four girls. Out of how many hundreds that we've employed?

ROEDER. Six, seven hundred. Over the years.

LEE. And some of them were sick when they got here. One girl you hired was a complete cripple. Couldn't even climb the stairs. Her father carried her up to the studio every morning.

ROEDER. It didn't make any difference to me how she got up the stairs—she was a fast worker and a very sweet little girl.

LEE. But she was in poor health.

ROEDER. She needed the work.

MARKLEY. Arthur. Charlie.

ROEDER. And not just for the money. To feel productive. To have a purpose. That's what work does, Charlie. It gives us a purpose. I don't see any reason why we should stop hiring girls like that.

LEE. When they get sick and try to blame us for it—you might want to reconsider that policy.

ROEDER. Let's see what Dr. Drinker has to say.

MARKLEY. Dr. Drinker?

LEE. Some professor at the Harvard School of Industrial Hygiene.

ROEDER. He chairs the department. And he's agreed to take a look at our operations.

LEE. Don't you think we're jumping the gun a bit, hiring him?

ROEDER. We've had six girls quit this week. And Mrs. MacNeil tells me there could be more.

LEE. Girls come and go all the time.

ROEDER. It's never been like this. These girls are terrified. We've got to do something to calm them.

LEE. Letting Drinker examine them? That sounds to me like a recipe for mass hysteria.

ROEDER. We'll tell them it's a routine physical. Edward?

MARKLEY. Companies give physicals all the time.

ROEDER. Then Drinker will start next month.

MARKLEY. In the meantime, I recommend we make an offer to Miss Kuser.

ROEDER. Settle?

LEE. There's no proof her problems are connected to us.

MARKLEY. If she sues—believe me, you won't like the publicity it brings. And neither will your investors.

LEE. You think this will affect the stock offering?

MARKLEY. Don't you?

ROEDER. Wonderful. We'll open at thirty and close at ten.

MARKLEY. Or not open at all.

LEE. But if we give this girl something—that will keep her quiet?

MARKLEY. It would be a condition of the settlement.

LEE. Maybe we better do it.

ROEDER. Suppose that lawyer has a racket going? He finds sick girls and talks them into making suits. Then we reward him for his larceny.

LEE. Unless...Miss Kuser genuinely believes she got sick here.

MARKLEY. It could be like Charlie said. She comes from a large, immigrant family. Not well educated. Not a lot of resources.

LEE. A few hundred dollars would make a big difference to a girl like that.

MARKLEY. Certainly. Pay a few doctor's bills. Buy some medicine. From the sound of that letter, I don't think the girl has long to live anyway.

ROEDER. So it would be a gesture of decency, then.

MARKLEY. Exactly.

ROEDER. What do you think we should offer?

(ROEDER sits down. Cross to:)

SCENE 6

(Enter REPORTER and SOB SISTER.)

REPORTER. March 24, 1924. Jack Youngwood here for the Newark Ledger.

SOB SISTER. Nancy Jane Harlan for the New York Graphic. The Graphic's only girl reporter!

REPORTER. Could radium water pose a cure for crippling arthritis? Scientific studies suggest a connection.

SOB SISTER. Dateline: Orange, New Jersey. Radium water products offer a miracle cure for crippling arthritis!

REPORTER. Some patients reported a significant abatement in their symptoms.

SOB SISTER. Mrs. Jeremy Michaels of the Bronx tells how radium water transformed her life!

MRS. MICHAELS. My pain got so bad I couldn't hardly bend over!

REPORTER. While others reported only mild relief.

SOB SISTER. This poor, brave woman could not even bend down to kiss her little ones good night.

MRS. MICHAELS. And I got three! Let me tell you! They are a handful.

REPORTER. Dr. Harrison Martland, chief medical examiner for Essex County, commented on the study.

MARTLAND. Preliminary at best.

REPORTER. Your recommendations, Dr. Martland?

MARTLAND. I advise— Further study. Further study. *(MARTLAND, REPORTER are distracted by the melodrama.)*

SOB SISTER. Then Mrs. Michaels tried Radithor!

MRS. MICHAELS. They said it would help my rheumatism, so I drank a bottle a day for a month. Wasn't cheap—but I was desperate.

MARTLAND. The test sample is questionably small.

MRS. MICHAELS. Well, first off, I felt like I been hit by a bolt of lightning, it was that powerful. Now I drink a bottle a week, just to maintain my health. I hang laundry and scrub the kitchen floor same way I always done.

REPORTER. Dr. William J.A. Bailey of Orange, inventor of Radithor, reports strong demand for his product.

SOB SISTER. Dr. William Bailey of Orange announces sales of Radithor exceed one hundred thousand cases worldwide!!

(Enter BAILEY, handing out bottles.)

BAILEY. Radioactivity is one of the most remarkable agents in medical science. I drink Radithor myself and I can vouch for its power.

MARTLAND. A bottle a day?

REPORTER. At a dollar a bottle?

MRS. MICHAELS. Worth every penny!

BAILEY. Yes, indeed. I myself was the picture of lethargy before I discovered the amazing, vitalizing qualities of radium water. Now look at me—I'm nearly fifty years old—but I have the energy of a man in his thirties.

SOB SISTER. You rather look like a man in his thirties.

BAILEY. Well. Thanks.

REPORTER. A testament to the tonic's potency?

MARTLAND. Or to the seller's creativity.

BAILEY. Radithor! It is perpetual sunshine!

REPORTER. And a perpetual money machine for its inventor.

SOB SISTER. Is there no end to what science can do?

(Cross to:)

SCENE 7

(The health department. A clock ticking, the tick of an interminable wait. GRACE waits. TOM waits. KATHRYN paces.)

GRACE. Maybe we shoulda made an appointment.

KATHRYN. Don't need no appointment.

GRACE. But it's a busy place, Kathryn. If you don't have an appointment, maybe you should make one.

KATHRYN. I shouldn't need no appointment for this!

(CLERK enters.)

CLERK. I'm sorry. I don't find anything under Schaub.

KATHRYN. No. It's under Rudolph.

CLERK. Rudolph?

KATHRYN. The girl I'm askin' about—Irene Rudolph.

CLERK. Did she file the complaint?

KATHRYN. NO! The dentist did!

CLERK. The dentist?

KATHRYN. Dr. Knef. Irene's dentist. He said she might have phossy jaw and he was going to complain to the health department about it. But when I asked him, he said he hadn't heard nothin', and it's been more than six months now!

CLERK. Phossy jaw, you say?

KATHRYN. YES! *(CLERK exits.)*

GRACE. Kathryn. It coulda been like your doctor said. A blood infection.

KATHRYN. Yeah, but what gave it to her? That's the thing. What was it from?

TOM. From dirt. You get infections from dirt.

KATHRYN. From dirt? Her face puffed up like a pumpkin. Her jaw rotted so bad, she couldn't eat nothin'. You think you get somethin' like that from a little dirt? You get it from phosphorous. They're tellin' everybody it's radium in that paint, but it's really phosphorous that makes it glow!

GRACE. Oh honestly, Kathryn. You can't really believe that.

KATHRYN. You saw her, Grace.

TOM. Kathryn, if it was like you say, they'da never let you work up there in the first place.

GRACE. Sure. They'da shut the place down.

KATHRYN. Shut it down? Who? Who's gonna shut it down?

GRACE. I don't know. The county?

KATHRYN. Honestly, Grace, you are such a ninny.

TOM. Hey.

KATHRYN. How they gonna shut it down if they don't know about it? EVER THINK OF THAT?

TOM. Now come on!

GRACE. It's all right, Tommy.

TOM. She got no business talkin' to you that way.

GRACE. She's just upset.

TOM. Upset? She's gone around the bend. She probably thinks they're dumpin' arsenic in the drinkin' water, now. Next it'll be they're kidnapping babies and using them to stoke the furnace.

KATHRYN. Go ahead and laugh. You won't laugh so hard when it's you comin' in here six months from now askin' after Grace.

TOM. Aw fer cryin' out loud.

GRACE. Kathryn. It's just a toothache!

KATHRYN. Yeah? That's how it started for Irene. Just a toothache. You wait, Grace. You wait, you'll wake up one morning, your gums hurting so bad you won't be able to open your mouth. So weak and sick ya won't be able to stand up—

TOM (overlapping). Stop it, Kathryn.

KATHRYN. The pain so bad you won't be able to sleep. And your face so swollen you won't be able to stand the sight of yourself—

TOM. I SAID STOP IT! (She is silent.) Grace is fine. Right, Gracie?

(CLERK enters with a file.)

CLERK. Irene Rudolph?

KATHRYN. That's it.

CLERK. She worked at the radium plant?

KATHRYN. Yes ma'am.

CLERK (studies the file. Then). Nothing.

KATHRYN. Huh?

CLERK. The company is in full compliance with all state health and labor regulations. They ordered an analysis of the paint—

KATHRYN *(grabs the file)*. Let me see that!

CLERK. Miss! Really—

KATHRYN *(looking at the file)*. Who's Miss Young?

CLERK. That's the health officer. Miss—

KATHRYN. ...paint is harmless compound of radium and zinc...??

CLERK *(getting the file back)*. As I was saying, the analysis shows there's no phosphorous in the paint. There's no phosphorous anywhere in the plant.

GRACE. There. You see, Kathryn?

CLERK. Miss Young toured the plant herself. She found nothing amiss. I'm sorry. *(Exit CLERK with file.)*

TOM. Well. Guess we can get some lunch then.

KATHRYN. I'm gonna file another complaint.

TOM. They already did an investigation!

KATHRYN. I WANNA FILE ANOTHER COMPLAINT! *(She turns away.)*

TOM. Oh, brother.

GRACE. Kathryn. These folks. They're awful busy here.

KATHRYN. I wanna file another complaint.

GRACE. I just don't see what good this is gonna do, Kathryn. To make such a fuss this way.

KATHRYN. Grace. Three surgeries and they wanted to cut her again. She finally said no. She knew. What was left of her jaw rotted so bad, the smell was terrible. And, Grace. The worst of it is. I couldn't look at her. Irene was so afraid of being alone—but I left her alone. When she died it was the middle of the night, and nobody was with her.

(KATHRYN starts to cry. GRACE goes to the counter and rings for the CLERK. CLERK appears.)

GRACE. I'm sorry. Can we have another form? My friend would like to file another complaint.

CLERK. Another complaint? Is the girl still sick?

GRACE. No. She died. *(The news startles the CLERK.)*

CLERK. Wait right here.

(CLERK leaves. GRACE looks back to KATHRYN. Tableau, then cross to:)

SCENE 8

(The front porch of Roeder's house. Late afternoon. MRS. ROEDER enters with a pitcher of lemonade and several glasses on a tray. She sees something she doesn't like.)

MRS. ROEDER. Harriet! Harriet you'll come down from that tree at once.

HARRIET'S VOICE *(off)*. I'm waiting for Papa!

MRS. ROEDER. Fine! When he gets here I'll send him up after you!

HARRIET *(off)*. There he is! Papa! Papa!

(ROEDER enters, carrying several bottles of Radithor. He waves cheerfully to HARRIET.)

ROEDER. Harriet!

MRS. ROEDER. Harriet! Come down at once!

HARRIET. Papa! I can see clear to the church!

ROEDER *(laughs)*. Can you? Do you see your grandfather?

HARRIET. No. But I see the schoolhouse!

MRS. ROEDER. You think this is funny?

ROEDER. She's enjoying herself.

MRS. ROEDER. HARRIET!

ROEDER. Tell you what. If she has no one to shout to…she won't shout.

MRS. ROEDER. They can hear her all over the neighborhood.

ROEDER. Can they? *(He leads her to a seat on the porch.)*

MRS. ROEDER. When she comes down, I want you to speak to her.

ROEDER. She's nine years old, Diane.

MRS. ROEDER. I'm trying to raise a daughter, not a son.

ROEDER. Time is on your side. In another year or two, she'll lose all interest in trees…and develop a fascination with boys.

MRS. ROEDER. That's supposed to scare me.

ROEDER. And when that day comes, you'll be frantic. Because she no longer wants to climb trees.

MRS. ROEDER. What's this?

ROEDER. Something to give you vitality.

MRS. ROEDER. You think I need vitality?

ROEDER. That's what it says on the bottle.

MRS. ROEDER. Is it pure?

ROEDER. We're his supplier. Want to try it?

MRS. ROEDER. If it will give me vitality—how could I refuse? *(He opens a bottle and pours a glass for her. A beat as she tastes it. She smiles her approval.)* Your father came by to see me today.

ROEDER. Another hard-luck case.

MRS. ROEDER. Four children at home. All under the age of six.

ROEDER. Let me guess—wife in the hospital with cancer.

MRS. ROEDER. Yes.

ROEDER. And the husband's been laid off from, let's see—the brickyard.

MRS. ROEDER. Yes!

ROEDER. Through no fault of his own.

MRS. ROEDER. How did you know?

ROEDER. Dad was around to see me yesterday. It's never enough with him. Just to have ordinary ambitions. You have to have a mission in life.

MRS. ROEDER. And you do.

ROEDER. No, I have a business plan.

MRS. ROEDER. You can't tell me you wouldn't help this man if you could.

ROEDER. If I could. But I can't give him a job that doesn't exist.

MRS. ROEDER. What about Dan Lehman?

ROEDER. Dan?

MRS. ROEDER. Maybe he could use some help.

ROEDER. In the laboratory? Dan needs trained technicians—not a bricklayer. Why don't you send him to Mrs. Middleton. Don't you women have a social club for things like this?

MRS. ROEDER. You mean the Women's Club civics committee?

ROEDER. Right.

MRS. ROEDER. Yes, the club takes an interest in such cases. But we're not an employment service, either. Which is why I thought you could help him.

ROEDER. Oh, you do love being married to the company president.

MRS. ROEDER. It has its advantages.

ROEDER. Ever think of trading it in?

MRS. ROEDER. Do you?

ROEDER. I got my shoes shined this morning. And while I sat there and watched the boy work, I thought: this is quite an enterprise. The work walks in, the work walks out. No inventory, no warehouse, no health inspectors, no stock price—

MRS. ROEDER. And you'll trade all of it in for your own shoeshine stand!

ROEDER. Fewer headaches that way.

MRS. ROEDER. So you're in one of those moods again! What is it this time? It can't be the market. It went up today!

ROEDER. Now you're reading the financial pages.

MRS. ROEDER. I have to entertain myself somehow. So what happened today? You're being very strange.

ROEDER. Am I? I'm sorry.

MRS. ROEDER. You can tell me, you know.

ROEDER. Nothing to tell. Really. This is going to be our best year ever.

MRS. ROEDER. So it's the prospect of success that you find so disheartening.

ROEDER. I'll get my checkbook.

MRS. ROEDER. What for?

ROEDER. Your bricklayer.

MRS. ROEDER. Artie! He needs a job, not charity. What is it your father says? A working man needs to work. It wears—

ROEDER *(overlapping)*. It wears on his soul not to work.
Well. If it's a matter of his soul. That's different. All
right. I'll have him talk to Dan.
MRS. ROEDER. Artie!
ROEDER. But I make no promises, Diane.
MRS. ROEDER. No promises.
ROEDER. To your health.

(They touch glasses and drink. Cross to:)

SCENE 9

(Dr. Knef's dental office. KNEF is examining GRACE.)

KNEF. How long you had this drainage?
GRACE. A week or two. Hurts somethin' awful, Dr. Knef.
KNEF. Anything else botherin' you?
GRACE. Back hurts some, too.
KNEF. Yer back now? You seen yer regular doctor?
GRACE. He says it's nerves.
KNEF. Nerves?
GRACE. About my weddin' and all.
KNEF. This ain't no case of nerves. Hope you told him
that.
GRACE. What do you think?
KNEF. Think you better schedule that surgery.
GRACE. Couldn't... Couldn't we put it off a little? Till af-
ter my weddin'?
KNEF. You don't have that surgery, you won't have no
weddin'.
GRACE. Huh?

KNEF. Miss Fryer. I want you to listen to me. Your jawbone is decaying. That's the black pus, oozing out of yer
gums. It's the bone itself.

GRACE. That's impossible!

*(Enter ROEDER, opposite, with a piece of long-awaited
mail. He opens it to read, and DRINKER appears.)*

DRINKER. To Mr. Arthur Roeder. U.S. Radium Corporation. From Cecil Drinker, Harvard University. Enclosed
is our report.

ROEDER. Finally!

DRINKER. We believe the trouble in your plant is due to
the radium.

ROEDER. Radium?

GRACE. I—it can't be as bad as all that. *(ROEDER continues to read, appalled at what he sees.)*

ROEDER. This can't be.

KNEF. Put off the surgery and you will develop a septic
condition. It could be fatal.

DRINKER. The blood changes in your employees can be
explained on no other grounds.

GRACE. Everything I've got—I saved for my wedding.

DRINKER. Photographic films carried by employees show
heavy fogging...

KNEF. Well, I got a suggestion for ya.

DRINKER. ...and we suspect high levels of gamma radia-
tion throughout the plant.

KNEF. Go to the radium plant and explain your situation.

GRACE. Go to the company?

DRINKER. We realize no proof can be offered at present...

KNEF. Once they see what kinda shape yer in...

ROEDER. This is impossible!

KNEF. ...They gotta feel obligated to help ya out.

DRINKER. But in view of the material in the literature...

ROEDER. It's a mistake.

DRINKER. ...and the facts disclosed by our investigation...

KNEF. I don't see how they could refuse!

DRINKER. We recommend immediate—and drastic—re-
medial action. *(Lights down on DRINKER.)*

KNEF. Look, if you want, I'll write to 'em for ya. They
can work through me, just pay my bills directly.

GRACE. You think they'd do that?

ROEDER. CHARLIE!

KNEF. They got a moral obligation, don't ya think?

GRACE. I guess so.

KNEF. We'll do it right now. I'll get some paper. *(Lights
down on GRACE and KNEF. ROEDER flips through the
report looking for anything hopeful.)*

ROEDER. He has to be wrong, that's all. He's wrong.

(Enter LEE.)

ROEDER. Charlie. *(He shows him the report.)* He has to
be wrong.

LEE. He must have overlooked something.

ROEDER. If we're suffering from a new ailment caused by
radium it should occur generally throughout the plant.

LEE. One would expect.

ROEDER. Several hundred milligrams are in solution at all
times in the big vats, several hundred milligrams in the
ore, several hundred in crystallizing.

LEE. The entire back yard is filled with tailings.

ROEDER. Radium is present in good amounts all over the property.

LEE. If it's the radium, then the incidence of illness should be highest in the laboratory.

ROEDER. And no one there is sick.

LEE. Then perhaps it's some combination of the radium with the zinc.

ROEDER. Or something peculiar to our plant alone.

LEE. Some kind of bacteria, perhaps? In the brushes?

ROEDER. It can't be the radium. There are dozens of application plants across the country. And none has ever reported anything like this.

LEE. The Department of Labor wants to see the report.

ROEDER. Yes I'm aware.

LEE. What are we going to do? This tears us to pieces. How do we answer them?

ROEDER. They want to see the report. *(ROEDER flips through, looking for a particular page that shows the company in the most favorable light. Then he tears the page out of the report and holds it out to LEE.)* We'll send them this.

LEE. One page?

ROEDER. The most important page. *(His meaning slowly sinks in to LEE.)*

LEE. Drinker will never stand for this.

ROEDER. Drinker works for us. This is a proprietary report. What we do with it is our business.

LEE. But the Department of Labor, Arthur.

ROEDER. We just need time, Charlie. Just a little time.

LEE. They could shut us down for this!

ROEDER. Scientists! Government men! They have no idea what it takes to run a business. Von Sochocky thought advertising was a dirty word. He laughed at the very idea of promotion. I can't tell you how many times I walked into that man's office and he turned a deaf ear to everything I told him. But, Charlie, we showed him. We showed him! Look at us. We are the world's largest single supplier of radium. The largest in the world. You know what it took for us to get here! Do you think I am going to stand idly by and let our good name be dragged through the mud? *(He holds out the paper to LEE.)* Trust me, Charlie.

(LEE takes the page and leaves. Shaken, ROEDER takes a moment to compose himself as crossfade to:)

SCENE 10

(Grace's house. Some months later. Her condition has worsened. She welcomes DR. FREDERICK FLINN, a fifty-something academic, warm and friendly, whose credentials are not immediately apparent to her.)

GRACE. Dr. Flinn, it's awful nice of you to come all this way.

FLINN. Not at all, my dear, not at all.

GRACE. I told the surgeon you was comin' over here, so he gave me the results of my blood work.

FLINN. Excellent! *(He looks over the papers.)*

GRACE. And, so?

FLINN. I must say, Miss Fryer. Your blood looks better than mine.

GRACE. It does?

FLINN. That's what happens to an old man who smokes. Now, tell me what else is troubling you.

GRACE. My feet and my back, mostly. I've had to wear a brace for a while.

FLINN. So I see. And this started before you left the company, or after?

GRACE. After I left. Dr. Knef says this all has to do with the radium plant. I know another girl from the plant who died from it. Irene Rudolph?

FLINN. Oh, yes! Terrible thing. Vincent's angina.

GRACE. What's that?

FLINN. That's an ulcerated condition of the mouth, my dear.

GRACE. From the radium?

FLINN. Oh, no, no, no. An unfortunate and rare result of poor dental care. So let this be a lesson to you: Always brush your teeth.

GRACE. There was something else in the paper about this— About other girls who got sick—one girl I worked with for a while—she's in the hospital in New York and the doctors don't know what to do. They never seen anything like it—

FLINN. Miss Fryer! Don't tell me you pay any attention to the papers! Those stories are not scientific!

GRACE. But—

FLINN. Reporters are not scientific. They do not follow scientific methods. They write to sell, not to educate. The scientist is not concerned with what sells. He is concerned with the truth. He undertakes years of painstaking study to arrive at an understanding of intricate natural processes that most people could never presume to comprehend! You would do well to listen to science and ignore the nonsense that is printed in the newspapers. Because I can tell you right now—radium has nothing to do with what's ailing you.

GRACE (*struggles to understand*). It doesn't?

FLINN. Not in the least.

GRACE. Then what is ailin' me?

FLINN. Poor diet, Miss Fryer. Poor diet.

GRACE. But Dr. Knef said—

FLINN. Dr. Knef is a dentist. Not a physician. What you have is a vitamin deficiency. You must eat more fresh fruit.

GRACE. Hard to do in the winter.

FLINN. And raw meat as well. That will help the anemia. Raw calves liver, particularly. Cook it if you must. But eat it twice a week. At a minimum. (*GRACE reaches for her wallet.*) No, no, no. I'm a scientist, Miss Fryer, and I take a purely scientific interest in this situation. By allowing me to examine you—you are helping me to advance my own studies. I thank you. (*He hands her a business card.*) Call me anytime. Day or night.

GRACE. Okay, Dr. Flinn. Thanks.

FLINN. Happy to be of service, my dear. (*GRACE shakes FLINN's hand and FLINN crosses to ROEDER in his office as GRACE studies the business card.*)

GRACE. Dr. Frederick Flinn, Ph.D. Physiology. Columbia University. (*The information troubles her.*) Ph.D.?

(*Enter KATHRYN, much sicker now.*)

GRACE. That's not a real doctor!

FLINN. My findings, Mr. Roeder.

KATHRYN. He's seen half a dozen girls used to work at the plant. Word I hear? He's workin' for the company!

ROEDER. An objective evaluation I trust?

FLINN. The source of my funding has no bearing on my research.

GRACE. And I let that fella examine me!

FLINN. I never examined her, per se. It was not a medical examination per se.

ROEDER. Nevertheless, you were able to offer her some useful advice?

FLINN. I did my best for her.

KATHRYN. Every girl he sees, it's the same thing: Nothin' wrong with ya.

GRACE. Yer blood is better than mine, he says!

ROEDER. And how are you doing on the rest of the report?

FLINN. The animal studies I conducted reveal no adverse affects from radium. The problem, as you suspected, is one of personal hygiene only.

GRACE. I can't believe somebody would do that. Straight out lie to ya like that.

KATHRYN. Nothin' surprises me.

GRACE. It's exactly the way you said, Kathryn. Those people will say anything. They'll do anything.

KATHRYN. Except the right thing.

GRACE. Well, we're gonna make 'em. Kathryn. We're gonna make sure someone hears about this. *(Exit KATHRYN and GRACE.)*

ROEDER. I am most grateful, Dr. Flinn. But I am particularly grateful to hear that the young lady you examined is doing so much better.

FLINN. Didn't examine her, no, no. I merely consulted with her.

ROEDER. All the same. She is doing much better, isn't that so?

FLINN. From what I could see, Mr. Roeder, she appears to be on the road to recovery.

ROEDER. Excellent!

FLINN. Here is my statement of fees and expenses.

ROEDER. Mr. Lee will draw you a check.

SCENE 11

(The Woman's Club of Orange. ENSEMBLE assembles to hear WILEY's speech. GRACE and TOM are at the back of the audience.)

WILEY. ...And so I leave you now with this one thought. Ladies and gentlemen: We do not have to accept injustice. We can use our powers as consumers to influence the practices of those who would wish to profit from our patronage. Thank you.

SOCIETYWOMAN. Thank you, Miss Wiley. And thanks to the New Jersey Consumer's League for another job well done! *(Applause from audience.)*

SOCIETYWOMAN. This concludes our program for this evening. I don't think we have time for questions. But we hope that you will join us next door for light refreshments! *(CROWD disperses.)*

TOM. You want anything?

GRACE. My throat's a little dry. *(He crosses off to get her a drink and GRACE spies her chance. She approaches*

WILEY, who is chatting with one of the guests, but GRACE is blocked by SOCIETYWOMAN.)

SOCIETYWOMAN. Can I help you, miss?

GRACE. I'm here to see Miss Wiley.

SOCIETYWOMAN. You're not a member of the Woman's Club.

GRACE. No, ma'am—

SOCIETYWOMAN. Are you a guest of a member?

GRACE. No, ma'am, but Miss Wiley—

SOCIETYWOMAN. Then I'm sure Miss Wiley would be happy to see you during her regular business hours.

GRACE. I'm not leavin' till I see Miss Wiley!

WILEY *(crosses to her).* It's all right, Mrs. Middleton. It's fine. *(Exit SOCIETYWOMAN.)* You must be Miss Fryer.

GRACE. Yes, ma'am. Miss Young at the health department said I should see you. I know I shoulda stopped by yer office, but I missed a lot of work lately and didn't want to miss no more.

WILEY. No need to apologize. I had been meaning to call on you myself. Please. Sit down.

GRACE. Me and Kathryn, we wrote to the company about our troubles, but we never heard nothing. So then we went to see a couple lawyers. But they all said they can't do anything, 'cause it's been so long since we left the radium plant. Something about the law won't allow it.

WILEY. The statute of limitations.

GRACE. Right. And one lawyer, he said he would try to sue anyhow, only he wants a thousand dollars up front! I already spent everything I saved for my wedding on doctors and dentists and hospitals. An' I still don't know. What's wrong. Exactly. And Tom—that's my

fella—he says he don't care! He wants to get married
anyhow. But I just wonder—what good would I do him,
like this? Miss Wiley. If I could just get some compensation, I could settle my debts—and then maybe I
wouldn't feel like I was saddling Tom with such a bur-
den... I'm sorry to rattle on at ya about these things...
I'm just so tired of bein' pushed around.

WILEY. I don't blame you.

GRACE. Miss Young at the health department, she said the
Consumer's League has—what did she say? Clout?

WILEY. I'd like to think so. We've certainly had our share
of successes.

GRACE. Can ya help us then?

WILEY. Tell me, Miss Fryer, just how far are you willing
to go with this?

GRACE. Ma'am?

WILEY. Suppose I do find a lawyer to take your case.
Someone willing to take it on a contingency—you
wouldn't have to pay him unless you won. Would you
be willing to sue?

GRACE. I want my compensation.

WILEY. Of course you do. Now suppose the company
says, "Here. Here's some money for you, Miss Fryer.
Only—you are to tell no one what we've agreed to. You
are to say nothing about how you got sick."

GRACE. Keep it quiet, you mean?

WILEY. Yes.

GRACE. That don't seem right.

WILEY. It isn't right. But that's what they'll do. They will
try to buy your silence. Is it for sale, Miss Fryer?

GRACE. No. No, ma'am, it isn't.

WILEY. Good.

(TOM returns with a glass of punch for GRACE. Seeing her in conference with WILEY, he takes a seat and waits.)

GRACE. So you will help us?

WILEY. I think I can help you. If you're willing to take some chances.

GRACE. Chances?

WILEY. Miss Fryer. If you would be willing to set aside your own need—just for the moment, we can put a stop to that company. We can stop them dead in their tracks.

GRACE. What do I have to do?

WILEY. We start by putting you on page one.

TOM. Page one? You want her to talk to the newspaper?

WILEY. Not just one newspaper. Many, many newspapers.

TOM. Is that really necessary? All we want is for Grace to get her compensation—

GRACE. Tommy. Let her finish.

WILEY. I understand your concerns. But this company has already shown it's willing to go to extremes to protect itself. No, I'm afraid the only way we'll get to them is to hit them where it matters most. Their public image. When every newspaper in America tells your story. How you were sorely treated. How you suffered. How the company denied all responsibility! Believe me, Miss Fryer, when that happens, Arthur Roeder will come to the table with his hat in his hands. *(GRACE looks to TOM. He nods.)*

GRACE. All right, Miss Wiley.

WILEY. I know it's a little frightening.

GRACE. It's okay. Right now, I'm more angry than I am scared.

WILEY. Good. You hang on to that anger, Miss Fryer. You're going to need it. Only—be sure no one else sees it.

GRACE. Ma'am?

WILEY. Public sympathy, Miss Fryer. That's our strongest weapon. And the public doesn't have much sympathy for an angry woman.

(Fade to black and:)

END ACT ONE

ACT TWO

SCENE 1

(A Sunday feature unfolds as WILEY observes.)

REPORTER. December 4, 1927! Jack Youngwood reporting for the Newark Ledger.

SOB SISTER. Nancy Jane Harlan for the New York Graphic!

REPORTER. On the strange case of the Radium Girls.

SOB SISTER. Who claim they were poisoned at the hands of their employer.

REPORTER. And now seek their day in court!

SHOPGIRL. Two hundred and fifty thousand dollars.

SOB SISTER. That's the price tag on their suffering!

MALE SHOPPER. Two hundred and fifty thousand dollars!

STORE OWNER. Ask me, it's all a sham!

CUSTOMER. What do you mean? Those girls are very sick!

STORE OWNER. Sicka workin', sure!

REPORTER. Doctors say...the Radium Girls have only a year to live!

SOB SISTER. Only one year to live and two hundred and fifty grand to spend! What would you do with that kind of money?

REPORTER. What would you do? To ease your last suffering days on earth? What would you do with two hundred and fifty thousand dollars?

SHOPGIRL. I'd buy a wardrobe like Irene Castle's.

CUSTOMER. I'd give it all to charity.

SHOPGIRL. Then I'd travel around the world—first class. With all my friends.

STORE OWNER. I'd play the stock market.

MALE SHOPPER. I'd buy my wife a fur coat and a diamond the size of New Hampshire.

(GRACE appears, walking with a cane.)

GRACE. I'd use it to pay my medical bills. *(Reaction from CROWD.)* And pay off the second mortgage on our house. The one my father took out to pay for my last operation. *(Reactions of sympathy.)*

SOB SISTER. Pretty Grace Fryer sits at home.

REPORTER. …suffering bravely through this entire ordeal.

SOB SISTER. …struggling valiantly to keep up her flagging spirits—

REPORTER. …for the sake of her family and her friends.

GRACE. It hurts to smile. But I try to smile. I know if I don't smile—I'll go crazy. *(Approval from the CROWD.)*

SOB SISTER. Tell us—Miss Fryer—how does it feel, knowing you have so little time left?

GRACE. I try not to think about it.

STORE OWNER. But it must get to ya sometimes—

CUSTOMER. Knowing what you've been through—

SHOPGIRL. And the company's gettin' fat off your labor!

MALE SHOPPER. And all they have to say about it is—

EVERYONE. No comment!

REPORTER. Don't you just wanna punch somebody?

GRACE. Oh, no. That won't do no good. I'd rather just think about...how it's gonna be. When justice prevails! Then I can do something nice for the folks. Maybe send 'em on a trip. They never did have no honeymoon.

SOB SISTER. What a fine example of womanhood! We can only aspire to bear our cross in life as nobly as this young girl.

(Applause from ensemble—GRACE blushes modestly. CROWD disperses as WILEY congratulates GRACE, then cross to:)

SCENE 2

(Berry's office. BERRY, MARKLEY and WILEY. MARKLEY is waving a newspaper.)

MARKLEY. Mr. Berry! I must object to this kind of histrionics.

BERRY. I had nothing to do with that, Mr. Markley.

MARKLEY. I've been in this game a long time, Mr. Berry. When I see a story like this...move over the wires. I am not so naive as to believe that a plaintiff's attorney has nothing to do with it.

BERRY. What's your proposal, Mr. Markley?

MARKLEY. Fifteen hundred dollars. For each girl.

BERRY. Fifteen hundred dollars?

WILEY. That's not even a year's wages!

MARKLEY. We think it's very generous. Considering your case won't survive the statute of limitations.

BERRY. This is a case in equity, sir. The chancery court will come to a different conclusion.

MARKLEY. The chancery court can't rewrite the law. And the law is clear: two years from the date of injury. Your clients are out of time.

BERRY. Two years from the date the *cause* of injury is discovered.

MARKLEY. Very creative, Mr. Berry. Very clever. I have to admire your imagination. But you've a long way to go before you convince the judge.

WILEY. And in the meantime, Mr. Markley—the press will continue to take a great interest in this story, and in the company's complete indifference to its workers.

MARKLEY. No doubt that will prove to be good press for the Consumer's League. And you accuse us of exploiting these girls.

WILEY. You're the one hiding behind the statute of limitations—

MARKLEY. Hiding Miss Wiley?

WILEY. You know very well the law never anticipated a situation like this. These girls were dying years before anyone knew the cause—

MARKLEY. Before *anyone* knew? Does that include the U.S. Radium Corporation, Miss Wiley? *(Barely able to keep from laughing.)* When—or I should say if—this case goes to trial, I only hope that's your opening argument, Mr. Berry. You will have made our defense. See you at the hearing. *(Exit MARKLEY.)*

WILEY. The arrogance of that man!

BERRY. Tell me again the purpose of these articles, Miss Wiley?

WILEY. Public sympathy, Mr. Berry. That's the engine of
    reform.

BERRY. You are antagonizing the company.

WILEY. Then the strategy is working.

BERRY. And what about the girls? How does it help them,
    to read in a dozen different newspapers that they have so
    little time to live?

WILEY. Mr. Berry. Surely you can see. The U.S. Radium
    Corporation cares nothing about the girls it has poi-
    soned—but the average housewife in Orange cares very
    deeply—and so do millions of other women across the
    country. These women shop. They buy watches.
    Markley can be as smug as he likes, but the Consumer's
    League campaign will lead to only one outcome—and
    he knows it. That is why he was here today.

BERRY. I only hope you're right, Miss Wiley.

WILEY. Public sympathy, Mr. Berry. Wait and see.

(Cross to:)

SCENE 3

(Lights up on an ELDERLY WIDOW.)

ELDERLY WIDOW. Dear Miss Schaub. I read of your sad
    story in the Boston Globe and am so sorry for your
    plight. It seems in this time of rapid advancement the
    well-being of the average worker is overlooked. I would
    like to share with you girls the key to my own good
    health at the age of ninety-two! It is called Christian Sci-
    ence.

(WIDOW freezes as lights up on:)

VENECINE SALESMAN. Dear Miss Fryer. I read of your woeful situation in the Atlanta Constitution and I am prepared to offer you a solution! VENECINE! A wonder tonic made from all natural ingredients, VENECINE will restore your health and vitality. We are prepared to offer you girls a lifetime supply of VENECINE in exchange for the *exclusive rights* to use your pictures in our advertisements.

(SALESMAN freezes as lights up on:)

LOVESICK COWBOY. Dear Girl. I read about you in the Billings Gazette. I run a hundred head of cattle up here and do very well by myself. I have always longed for a companion and am well equipped to offer you a comfortable home in your final hours. A girl like you has suffered so much— Don't you think you deserve a few fleeting hours of happiness? Sincerely, your admirer, Leonard F. Watkins. P.S. Enclosed is my picture.

(During above, scene has shifted to the hospital. When COWBOY finishes, lights go down on him and up immediately on GRACE, looking at the COWBOY's picture. She is in a hospital room, with KATHRYN.)

GRACE. Look at this, Kathryn! This man actually sent a picture. *(KATHRYN dabs her mouth with a handkerchief.)* Ya all right, Kathryn?
KATHRYN. Bleedin' again.
GRACE. Shall I get the nurse?

KATHRYN. It did this before. It'll stop.

GRACE. Maybe we should go.

KATHRYN. No, don't go!

GRACE. Don't ya need to sleep?

KATHRYN. Who can sleep? I never sleep.

GRACE. Well. You'll sleep tomorrow.

KATHRYN. Yeah. Might not wake up.

GRACE. 'Course you'll wake up.

KATHRYN. Not if it don't go well. Sometimes you don't come out of it so good...my mother's cousin, she went into the hospital for her appendix and she didn't come home again...

GRACE. Well, you just can't think that way. That's all. Look at this mail, Kathryn. Miss Wiley said folks would be on our side, and she sure was right. Here's one from California—

KATHRYN *(abruptly)*. What if we don't win?

GRACE. 'Course we'll win.

KATHRYN. But what if we don't? My father will lose his house. We'll be on the street. You'll be on the street, too. Yer father must owe thousands. And you and Tom, you won't never get married. How can ya stand it, Grace—

GRACE. Kathryn, please!

KATHRYN *(more agitated)*. How can Tom stand it? Don't ya ever wonder, Grace? I don't never hear him complain—

GRACE. Kathryn! As soon as the judge hears our testimony, he's gonna rule for us. All they gotta do is take one look at us. It'll be over in a day.

KATHRYN. Think so?

GRACE. Sure. When they see what kind of shape we're in. We'd be awful hard to ignore, don't you think?

KATHRYN. That'll be somethin' then, won't it? To see the look on Mr. Roeder's face, when we get on the stand?

GRACE. Now. You wanna read some more letters?

(Enter TOM with a brown paper bag.)

TOM. They didn't have no vanilla. So I got some chocolate.

GRACE. Took you long enough.

TOM. Don't get on me. I had six people stop me on the way over here—all of 'em reporters and all of 'em askin' after *you.*

KATHRYN *(trying to joke)*. Waitin' for me to die.

GRACE. No one is waitin' for you to die.

KATHRYN. It's true. One of 'em. Called my mother. Askin' if I had died. When she said "No," he sounded... disappointed.

GRACE. Try to eat a little of this. You'll feel better.

(A PHOTOGRAPHER and SOB SISTER make an unexpected entry.)

SOB SISTER. Evenin', girls! How about a picture? *(GRACE starts.)*

TOM. For the love of Mike! What are ya doin'!

SOB SISTER. We need some pictures for the Graphic's exclusive on the girls.

TOM. Exclusive? Whadda ya talkin' about?

SOB SISTER. Five thousand dollars, that's what. Whadda ya say, Grace? That sound good to you? Think you could use five thousand dollars?

GRACE. I don't understand.

SOB SISTER. Perhaps you're familiar with Benarr McFadden—

TOM. Who, that faith healer?

SOB SISTER. Herbalist, Mr. Kreider, herbalist! Benarr McFadden's patented herbal therapy is just the thing to get these girls back on their feet! And the Graphic will pay for it! All we ask is the exclusive rights to their story from here on out. See for yourself. *(She hands TOM a contract.)*

GRACE. You want to pay us? To go see Benarr McFadden?

PHOTOGRAPHER. Easy money, huh?

KATHRYN. Let me see.

TOM. They're serious, Grace.

SOB SISTER. The Graphic always does business on the up and up.

GRACE. I don't know.

TOM. Grace. What—what does your father owe on the house?

GRACE. I don't know exactly.

TOM. And that last hospital bill? That was a couple hundred at least.

GRACE. At least.

TOM. Maybe we should think about this.

KATHRYN. And all we do. Is talk. To this herbalist fella.

SOB SISTER. Of course, we'll have to get our money's worth—a regular series of features—with pictures—following the course of the treatment, your illness, recovery—or otherwise—depending on how it goes.

GRACE. And then you print whatever you want.

SOB SISTER. Maybe we add some color. Everybody adds color.

TOM. It don't sound so bad.

KATHRYN. Maybe. We should talk. To Miss Wiley. About it.

SOB SISTER. Miss Wiley! What's it to her? You're the ones with bills to pay.

GRACE. Wouldn't be right to do something like this. Without talking to Miss Wiley.

SOB SISTER. You're a big girl, Grace. Can't you make your own decisions?

GRACE. 'Course I can make my own decisions.

TOM. Ya'd take it if it came from the company.

GRACE. The company owes us a lot more than that.

TOM. If ya ever see it.

KATHRYN. Grace. Maybe we should do it.

GRACE. It just don't feel right.

TOM. You're gonna talk to them reporters anyhow. Why not get somethin' out of it?

SOB SISTER. He's right, ya know! Why give your story away when people are crazy to read it? Believe me, you girls could cash in big. The day we ran the feature on you—BANG! Sold out of every copy at every newsstand. Everybody can sympathize with the plight of some poor sick girl facing certain death—with no hope of fulfilment in motherhood. *(Her words are like a slap across the face.)*

GRACE. I'd like you to go now. My friend is tired. She needs her rest.

TOM. Grace. At least think about it. *(GRACE wheels KATHRYN off as TOM follows.)*

SOB SISTER. Sure. Think it over. I understand—you're worried about what people will say. But hey—you gotta think about your own interests here. There's no reason you shouldn't get something out of all of this. Look out for number one, that's the way. Everyone else is out to get what they can. For sure. Why should ya sit back and keep your nose clean when everyone else is up to their elbows in it?

SCENE 4

(Scene transforms to the U.S. Radium boardroom, a smoky backroom effect. DR. KNEF is making a proposal to the board, seated at a long table, largely in shadow. ROEDER at the opposite end. LEE, MARKLEY and members of the board are present.)

KNEF. Gentlemen. I have treated a number of the girls who claim they got sick here. One of them, the girl's jaw had rotted so bad I removed it just by lifting the bone out of her mouth. As you can see. *(He produces a specimen: a bone fragment in a jar of formaldehyde.)*

ROEDER. That's all right, Dr. Knef. You can put that away.

KNEF. Maybe you'd rather look at it on the x-ray. *(Producing the x-ray.)* This was an expensive case to treat and I never did get no compensation. The girl died. Her family never paid.

ROEDER. I sympathize Dr. Knef. But what has that to do with us?

KNEF. Here it is straight: There's going to be a lot more girls coming out and saying they got sick here. So maybe we can do business. I scratch your back, you scratch mine. That sort of thing.

ROEDER. I'm not following you.

KNEF. Suppose you was to give me a list of the girls who worked here. I'd see to it there weren't no more lawsuits.

ROEDER. You think you could cure them?

KNEF. I couldn't put out a cure, no. I'm saying—I scratch your back, you scratch mine.

BOARD #1. How so, Dr. Knef?

KNEF. I'd examine them for radium necrosis, and then I would come up with a favorable diagnosis for you—pyorrhea, say, or something else. Quite a few cases will just die a natural death anyway—and the rest we can put off for a while until the statute of limitations kicks in and it's too late to sue.

MARKLEY. You'll persuade them they haven't got a case against the company?

KNEF. Exactly. And if it did come to court—I could testify that it was some other problem. And it would be strong testimony coming from the dentist who treated them.

ROEDER. What makes you so sure these girls will come to you?

KNEF. They'll come to me quick if I don't charge 'em nothing.

ROEDER. Because we'd be paying you.

KNEF. Exactly right. We understand each other, Mr. Roeder.

MARKLEY. Exactly what are you asking for, Dr. Knef?

KNEF. I'd need ten thousand dollars—for my troubles so far, and for every girl I'd agree to see from here on out, two dollars for every visit, plus expenses for the x-rays. I'm suggesting a gentleman's agreement here—better off if it's not in writing.

ROEDER. No.

KNEF. All right, we'll put it in writing—

ROEDER. We'll do nothing of the kind. Your proposal is immoral and we'll have nothing to do with it.

KNEF. Immoral you say? You're a fine one to be talkin' about morals.

ROEDER. Mr. Lee—

KNEF. When you got your own hired guns, ready to testify—

ROEDER. Those are expert witnesses.

KNEF. Expert witnesses? Paid lackeys is more like it. And none of 'em's got the dirt I got. If you're smart, you'll play ball with me. Believe me. There's plenty of other folks interested in the information...

ROEDER. You're threatening me.

KNEF. Just a business proposition, Mr. Roeder. Just lookin' out for my interests—same way you look after yours.

ROEDER. Mr. Lee! See Dr. Knef to the door.

KNEF. All right, all right! You don't want to play ball—Fine. But believe me. When all this shakes out, it won't be me holding the short end of the stick. *(Exit KNEF.)*

ROEDER. Gentlemen, I want you all to make statements on what happened this morning. We'll send them to the State Dental Society. Then Dr. Knef will see who's playing ball and who isn't.

BOARD #2. An excellent idea. *(Muttered agreement.)*

BOARD #1. I don't know. Perhaps we shouldn't be so quick to dismiss Knef's proposal.

ROEDER. What do you mean?

BOARD #1. We're in a very bad situation here, Mr. Roeder.

BOARD #3. That's true. Mr. Lee says you're having trouble getting girls to work here—

LEE. Yes, and we've lost some contracts because of it.

BOARD #3. And it's going to get worse.

BOARD #1. The papers are full of stories about those girls...

LEE. Making them out to be saints.

BOARD #1. And what defense can we put out?

LEE. Except to say we'll try our case in court.

BOARD #1. And in the court of public opinion, we've already lost!

BOARD #2. Perhaps we should reconsider. It certainly wouldn't hurt to have testimony from a dentist who treated those girls.

BOARD #1. Knef could be very helpful to us. We should retain him.

ROEDER. Retain him as what? An extortionist?

BOARD #1. As an expert.

BOARD #3. Like Dr. Flinn.

ROEDER. Dr. Flinn is a highly respected professor at Columbia University. Knef is a neighborhood dentist.

BOARD #2. But Dr. Flinn treated some of the girls, didn't he?

ROEDER. He didn't treat them. He consulted with them.

LEE. He dispensed medical advice, Arthur.

ROEDER. It wasn't medical advice. It was an expert's opinion—a scientific opinion. *(A pause as the BOARD considers.)*

BOARD #1. How about this? We retain Knef, but we don't put him on the stand. Just so we keep him from testifying for the women.

BOARD #3. That's the most important thing.

BOARD #2. Yes, I agree. That's the most important thing.

BOARD #1. Would you agree to something like that, Mr. Roeder?

BOARD #2. Mr. Roeder?

BOARD #3. Mr. Roeder?

ROEDER *(can't believe what he is hearing)*. Edward! We can't possibly do this. We can't get into bed with a man like Knef! *(A beat.)*

MARKLEY. Arthur's right. We don't want to do business with Knef.

LEE. He could hurt us. We have to take steps.

MARKLEY. Knef has already given us everything we need. *(Holding up the x-rays.)* New evidence, gentlemen. This is grounds for a postponement.

(Tableau, then cross to:)

SCENE 5

(A room in the Essex County Courthouse. BERRY and WILEY.)

BERRY. Three months! Three months to study an x-ray. It's outrageous! And the girls! Did you see the girls? Their eyes were like saucers, looking at me. Terrified.

WILEY. Mr. Berry—

BERRY. How are they going to hold out three more months? Kathryn Schaub could barely make it into the courtroom today! And Grace. She was trying so hard not to cry. And of course I had all the answers. "Go home, girls. Get some rest." That's the best I can do. "Get some rest."

WILEY. You're doing wonderfully, Mr. Berry. It's a difficult case—

BERRY. I don't understand people like Markley. And Roeder? How can he play this kind of game? With those poor girls sitting right there!

WILEY *(retrieving a document from her briefcase)*. Maybe this will help to explain. I received a letter—

BERRY. You'd think the company would be eager to take care of this! With the kind of publicity this has gotten. But Markley seems to enjoy the sport of it. What he can get away with. It's cold. Very cold.

WILEY. Mr. Berry. *(She extends a document.)*

BERRY. What's this?

WILEY. It's from Kathryn Drinker. Mrs. Cecil Drinker? Of Harvard? She's an industrial hygienist also. She worked with Dr. Drinker on his study of the radium plant. It was a joint effort, actually.

BERRY. That's very interesting, Miss Wiley. But we've already seen that document. There's nothing in it to help us.

WILEY. You've only seen part of it, Mr. Berry. Please. *(She slides the report across the table.)* This is the complete report. *(BERRY looks it over.)* I received it this morning. Mrs Drinker has been following our story very closely in the papers. And she was particularly disturbed to read that last article in the Ledger, the one where Mr. Lee says her study "clears" the company.

BERRY. He doctored the report. Roeder doctored the report.

WILEY. Apparently he pulled out one page listing the blood conditions of a dozen employees and passed it off as the whole thing. Doesn't look so bad by itself, does it? But in context…it's a somewhat…different picture.

BERRY. We can use this.

WILEY. Yes. That should impress the judge.

BERRY. The judge? Miss Wiley. I am not going to wait three months to make use of this. I want you to call that contact you have at the New York World. If Roeder won't let us present our evidence in the courtoom, then he can read about it in the newspaper.

SCENE 6

(Enter SOB SISTER and REPORTER.)

REPORTER. Jan. 12, 1928! Jack Youngwood reporting for the Newark Ledger!

SOB SISTER. Nancy Jane Harlan for the Graphic!

REPORTER. Radium Girls Go to Court Today!

SOB SISTER. Radium Girls Knock at the Doors of Justice! Will they be heard?

REPORTER. These poor injured girls face pain!

SOB SISTER. Disfigurement!

REPORTER. Ruin!

SOB SISTER *(cheerfully)*. And death! And as the clock ticks away the precious moments…

REPORTER. A hearing begins in chancery court!

SOB SISTER. Where the U.S. Radium Corporation demands a postponement—

REPORTER. While plaintiff's attorney Raymond Berry makes a shocking disclosure!

SOB SISTER. Showing that the company lied to the Department of Labor!

REPORTER. Showing that it distorted the results of a Harvard study!

SOB SISTER. Concealing the ill effects of its product!

REPORTER. Read all about it in the Ledger!

SOB SISTER. Read it in the Graphic! We care. Because you care.

(Above covers transition to:)

SCENE 7

(The parlor in Roeder's house. MRS. ROEDER is reading a newspaper as ROEDER enters with a bottle of Radithor and pours out two glasses—as if drinking it has become a nightly ritual.)

ROEDER. Very bad?

MRS. ROEDER. You didn't read it?

ROEDER. I make a point not to, these days.

MRS. ROEDER. If only other people would do the same. Mrs. Mitchell from across the street. She walked right past me this morning, didn't say a word to me. I know she saw me. And the women at the market. And the green grocer...the way they glance at each other...and at the club, Mrs. Middleton and the other ladies. The whispers.

ROEDER. Why don't you put that away? Read the Journal.
I saw it here the other day. Why don't you read that?

MRS. ROEDER *(overlapping)*. At the club today, someone
actually had the nerve to say to me: Is it true? Is it true,
she said? Did your husband poison those women? I said:
"Mrs. Cowles. If you think it is true, then why would
you speak to me at all? I certainly would not associate
with a woman whose husband did such things."

ROEDER. Why do you go there, then? If that's the way
people are.

MRS. ROEDER. I've been a member for years.

ROEDER. What do you want me to say, Diane? I knew we
were poisoning people, but we didn't want to stop because we were making too much money. Is that what
you want me to say?

MRS. ROEDER. I certainly don't want you to say such a
thing.

ROEDER. Even if it were true? *(A silence. In the silence
lies a suspicion that ROEDER has never felt before.)* Or
especially if it were true?

MRS. ROEDER. Is it true?

ROEDER. Is that what you think?

MRS. ROEDER. What would you like me to think?

ROEDER. For God's sakes, Diane. Don't you see what's
going on? It's Von Sochocky. He's behind all this. He's
jealous of our success. He's feeding information to the
Consumer's League—so they can railroad us.

MRS. ROEDER. Why would the Consumer's League—

ROEDER. Bunch of radical women—do-gooders—half of
them are Reds probably—Socialists! That's what they
are. Same thing with that club you belong to.

MRS. ROEDER. What?

ROEDER. You women think you can go around and fix the world's problems.

MRS. ROEDER *(overlapping)*. I can't. I'm sorry—

ROEDER *(overlapping)*. —while your husbands go out and make a living. You're going to quit that club.

MRS. ROEDER. Quit the club!

ROEDER. And stop talking to that idiot Mrs. Middleton. // She doesn't know anything.

MRS. ROEDER *(overlapping on //)*. You're not making any sense.

ROEDER. None of those women know anything!! You don't know anything. *(Silence.)*

MRS. ROEDER *(quiet determination)*. Did you lie to the Department of Labor?

ROEDER. What? *(MRS. ROEDER holds out the newspaper. He takes it, looks at it.)*

MRS. ROEDER. Did you lie?

ROEDER. I didn't lie. I just... Didn't agree with Drinker's results.

MRS. ROEDER. Arthur.

ROEDER. I have a fiduciary duty to the company.

MRS. ROEDER. I can't listen to this.

ROEDER. Diane! I have documents— I have articles— People with tumors the size of baseballs. Radium therapy—the tumors disappear. Diane.

MRS. ROEDER. I'm tired. I'm going upstairs.

ROEDER. We save lives. We make lives better—mild radium therapy—invigorates. You can't really think I'm a liar. Diane. You can't really believe I would set out to poison people. Can you? Diane?

MRS. ROEDER. No.

ROEDER. Do you think I would ever do anything to hurt you? Or to hurt Harriet?

MRS. ROEDER. Certainly not.

ROEDER. Then?

MRS. ROEDER. Thirteen girls have died.

ROEDER. People die every day. The newspapers are full of death notices—young, old—infants. Children, younger than Harriet. Die every day.

MRS. ROEDER. But they worked for you!

ROEDER. They also worked other places. Diane. I have a report from Columbia University—an expert in industrial hygiene, just like Drinker—who says there is no connection between our plant and these illnesses. Would you like to see the report?

MRS. ROEDER. Then. What...what could the cause be?

ROEDER. I don't know. Diane. I really don't know. I've done everything I could to find out. No one knows. *(Beat.)* Please say you believe me. If you don't believe me, there's no point to anything.

MRS. ROEDER. Artie. *(She goes to him. With relief he embraces her.)*

ROEDER. You remember the day I told my father I wasn't going into the ministry? What you said to me that day?

MRS.ROEDER. You can do as much good in a boardroom as you can in a church.

ROEDER. You remember.

MRS. ROEDER. You think I would forget?

ROEDER. I was such a scared kid. And he—he was an icon. If it weren't for you. I don't think I could have stood up to him.

MRS. ROEDER. I'm sure you would have, Artie. I know you would have.

ROEDER. And ever since then. He's been looking for signs. That my soul is lost. You don't think that, do you? That my soul is lost?

MRS. ROEDER. You're a good man, Artie.

ROEDER. We save lives, Diane.

MRS. ROEDER. You save lives. *(She retrieves the Radithor.)*

ROEDER. It's all for you. You know that, don't you? Everything I do. It always has been.

MRS. ROEDER. I know. *(They drink the Radithor. He takes her hand and kisses it. Doorbell rings.)*

ROEDER. Please don't let that be another reporter. *(Doorbell.)* Don't answer it. *(Doorbell.)*

LEE *(off)*. Arthur!

MRS. ROEDER. Is that Mr. Lee?

ROEDER *(gets the door)*. Charlie, for God's sakes—

LEE. I just got off the telephone with someone from the Ledger.

ROEDER. This couldn't wait until morning??

LEE. I'm sorry. Good evening.

MRS. ROEDER. Mr. Lee.

LEE. It's Dr. Lehman.

MRS. ROEDER. Dan?

LEE. He's dead, Arthur.

ROEDER. What?

LEE. He died this morning.

ROEDER. Charlie. That's not possible. I just saw him last week.

MRS. ROEDER. He was just here—a month ago. For cards—they were just here.

LEE. Martland's already done the autopsy. He says it was a severe anemia.

ROEDER. He's blaming the radium.

LEE. The Ledger is going to run it on page one. I told the
reporter we would issue a statement at eight o'clock.
That's when he needs it—so it can run tomorrow—

ROEDER. When are the services?

LEE. Sorry?

ROEDER. The services.

LEE. I don't know.

ROEDER. We'll send flowers. Diane?

MRS. ROEDER. Of course. I'll call Louise—

ROEDER. Yes, that's right—call Louise—

MRS. ROEDER. I should go over and see her. Oh poor
Louise. We should go see her right now.

LEE. I wouldn't do that.

MRS. ROEDER. Why ever not?

LEE. She's planning to sue.

ROEDER. Louise?

LEE. The reporter from the Ledger told me. She's filing a
wrongful-death action. *(Beat.)* I've worked up a statement for the paper. Company chemist for eight years...
always in poor health, recently in decline...

MRS. ROEDER. But Dan was never sickly. He was always
on the golf course...or sailing...or...their garden, Artie.
He kept a...a beautiful...garden.

ROEDER. Let's take care of this in the morning, Charlie.

LEE. Of course. Sorry to bring you the bad news, Mrs.
Roeder. Good night.

MRS. ROEDER. Good night, Mr. Lee. *(LEE exits.)*

ROEDER. Charlie can be a bit excessive at times. *(MRS.
ROEDER is silent as she picks up the Radithor.)* We
have to say something. I don't know what we'll say, but

we have to say something. The shareholders will expect it.

MRS. ROEDER. You needn't explain, Artie.

ROEDER. Sometimes it's necessary—

MRS. ROEDER. It's all right. You needn't explain. *(She gives him the Radithor.)* We're going to throw this away now.

ROEDER. There's half a case under the sink.

MRS. ROEDER. And we'll get rid of that, too. We'll have no more of it in the house.

ROEDER. I'll do it. *(MRS. ROEDER starts to go.)* Diane? *(A beat.)* I'm in too far to quit.

MRS. ROEDER. I really didn't expect you to.

(Cross to:)

SCENE 8

(DR. MARTLAND appears.)

MARTLAND. February 21, 1928. To: Mr. Raymond Berry. From: Harrison Martland. Medical Examiner, Essex County. We have examined the remains of the deceased Amelia Maggia. Our study reveals the following: Radioactive substances have been found in large quantities in the lower jaw, the upper jaw and the lumbar vertebrae. No evidence of syphilis was found.

(Enter REPORTER and SOB SISTER.)

REPORTER. Body is Radioactive!

SOB SISTER. Bones of Dead Girl Kick Off Gamma Rays!

REPORTER. Katherine Wiley of Consumer's League Declares: New Evidence Shows Company Lied.

(Enter WILEY.)

WILEY. Dr. Joseph Knef, a Newark dentist who treated Amelia, has turned over portions of the jawbone that he removed from her mouth. This x-ray film shows the jawbone is still radioactive five years after the girl died.

REPORTER. Will this make your case?

SOB SISTER. Will this force a settlement?

WILEY. Make our case? No—this gentleman will make our case.

SOB SISTER. Last night, in a Graphic exclusive...

(VON SOCHOCKY enters as REPORTER leaves in disgust.)

SOB SISTER. ...the founder of the Radium Corporation broke his long silence with this shocking announcement:

VON SOCHOCKY. Radium is one of the most dangerous substances known to man.

SOB SISTER. Dr. Von Sochocky! Is it true you assisted with the autopsy?

VON SOCHOCKY. Ya. And given my expertise in radium extraction, I was able to determine Miss Maggia absorbed enough radium to kill ten people.

SOB SISTER. Doctor! What does this say for mild radium therapy? Are you now advising against it?

VON SOCHOCKY. Radium is responsible for the deaths of these poor girls. It should be considered a most dangerous substance—

SOB SISTER. Do you agree with the doctor's prognosis? That the Radium Girls have only a year to live?

VON SOCHOCKY. From what I've seen. They'll be lucky to last that long.

(Cross to:)

SCENE 9

(Grace's house. GRACE is looking at dresses.)

TOM. I'll tell ya what we shoulda done. We shoulda took that reporter up on her offer when we had the chance. That's what we shoulda done.

GRACE. Five thousand dollars. Don't make me laugh.

TOM. We shoulda talked her up too—'cause I'll tell ya what—they'da paid. And I'll tell ya what else we shoulda done—

GRACE. Stop tellin' me what we shoulda done! Lots of things we shoulda done. It don't do no good to think about 'em now.

TOM. All right. Keep your shirt on.

GRACE. What do you think? The red or the blue?

TOM. So what's Berry say? Is he gonna go back to the company?

GRACE. I like the red, but it don't fit so good these days.

TOM. Is he gonna try to talk the company up a bit?

GRACE. Miss Wiley thinks another interview will do the job. So I say, what's one more? Ya know?

TOM. It's worth a try, don't you think? What if they came up to five thousand? Would ya take it then?

GRACE. Let 'em come up. I'm not cavin' in…

TOM. It's called a settlement.

GRACE. A settlement. It's a just a way for them to hide.

TOM. Let 'em hide.

GRACE. Then they win.

TOM. So they win. They're gonna win anyway.

GRACE. Nice you got so much confidence in me.

TOM. Grace, for Christ's sake. You got one lawyer workin' for nothin'—up against six other lawyers who are getting a bundle. And you think you got a chance?

GRACE. Y'know what I found out today? They put lead screens in the laboratory. For the technicians. Did they give us lead screens?

TOM. Oh Jesus.

GRACE. What d'ya think? One hundred girls in a room and they're gonna spend that kinda money on us?

TOM. Grace—

GRACE. And they want to keep it all quiet.

TOM. What are we doin' here, Grace?

GRACE *(overlapping)*. And Miss Wiley says they're gonna close down here.

TOM *(overlapping)*. Grace. Grace!

GRACE. And move across the river. To New York—to open up another factory. Like nothin' ever happened—

TOM. What are we doin' here! I thought the idea was ya'd get some money to settle your debts—get a better doctor—and we'd get on with things.

GRACE. Get on with things.

TOM. You're still wearin' my ring. *(His words yank her out of her tirade.)*

GRACE. Oh, Tommy.

TOM *(taking her hand)*. Grace. There's a house for sale in my brother's neighborhood— Two rooms up, two rooms down, not much, but it's a start. You'll like it. It's already got flowered wallpaper. And best of all—it's only three blocks from the school.

GRACE. The school? What do we need with a school?

TOM. Plan ahead for once. *(A beat.)*

GRACE. Tommy. What do you think is going to happen? After all this is over. D'ya think everything will just go back to the way it was?

TOM. Why wouldn't it? *(A pause.)*

GRACE. I gotta see the surgeon again.

TOM. Uh-huh.

GRACE. I got some fluid. He's gonna drain it.

TOM. Okay.

GRACE. And then, he says. There'll be more.

TOM. So we deal with it when it comes.

GRACE *(overlapping)*. —AND STILL MORE! and then more and still more—why can't you see that? How can you talk about buying houses and getting married when you know there's nothing— *(She stops herself.)*

TOM. Grace. I can't think about that. I just want for us to be together now. I want to come home to you at night. To my wife—my home. I'm too old to be living like this—this, in-between life. I promise, Grace. I'll do whatever it takes to make it easy for you. *(A silence. GRACE takes off her ring and holds it out to him.)*

GRACE. Here.

TOM. Grace. Come on.

GRACE. I shoulda give it back to you a long time ago.

TOM. I don't want it.

GRACE. Tommy. Please. Are ya gonna make me say it?

TOM. You just need to get some rest. That's all. You're not gettin' enough sleep. I'll be back to see you. tomorrow—

GRACE. Tommy!

TOM. You get some sleep.

GRACE. Tommy. Tommy! Don't you do this to me. TOMMY! *(He is gone.)*

SCENE 10

(The empty dialpainting studio. ROEDER sits alone as LEE passes.)

LEE. Arthur?

ROEDER. Ah, Charlie.

LEE. Aren't you headed home?

ROEDER. Charlie. I've been thinking it over. I think we're taking the wrong approach here. I think we should settle this case. We've got to make a reasonable offer to those girls.

LEE. No, Arthur. We agreed. We need a definitive victory. Otherwise we invite more of the same nonsense.

ROEDER. Things have changed.

LEE. Arthur. I know you and Dan were close. But you can't let that cloud your judgment.

ROEDER. Von Sochocky is going to testify.

LEE. We can deal with him.

ROEDER. How?

LEE. Put more money in his pocket.

ROEDER. Now you want to bribe him?

LEE. Not a bribe. Consideration.

ROEDER. Consideration.

LEE. For an expert witness. Whatever Berry is paying him—we'll just make a better offer.

ROEDER. You don't understand guilt, do you, Charlie?

LEE. Right now, I don't have the luxury of thinking about it.

ROEDER. Let me tell you something, Charlie. A guilty man—has a tremendous need to unburden himself. His guilt can eat him alive. Don't you see? What Von Sochocky wants is to be free. That is why he is testifying for the girls. That is why he will never testify for us. No matter how much consideration you offer.

LEE. Settle with these girls and you'll have to settle with all the others. Knef was right about that. This is just the beginning.

ROEDER. Tell Markley to get in touch with Berry. Get a conversation going. Come up with a figure the girls can accept.

LEE. Arthur, for God's sake! What are you trying to do to me? You want to wipe me out?

ROEDER. We've got to get this off the table.

LEE (overlapping). Every penny. Every penny I've put by in the last seven years I have sunk into this company. Why? Because of you. Because you said it was a sure thing. No miss—"why work for Von Sochocky when we can work for ourselves?" Remember that one? "Take a chance, Charlie. Take a chance!"

ROEDER. Charlie. We were fooled. Von Sochocky fooled us all. The only thing to do now is to try to clean it up as best we can.

LEE. Do this, and it's the end, Arthur.

ROEDER. You're stepping down, Charlie?

LEE. Not me. (A silence.)

ROEDER. Well.

LEE. Don't you know? They are one vote away from getting rid of you.

ROEDER. And whose vote is that, Charlie?

LEE. Arthur. Have you so little faith in me?

ROEDER. I'm still a stockholder, Charlie. You don't have enough votes to get me off the board. I'll still be on the board.

LEE. And still on the hook if this company goes under. Think about that the next time your conscience starts to bother you.

(Exit LEE. Fade on ROEDER. Lights rise on MARKLEY.)

MARKLEY. March 15, 1928. To Raymond Berry, attorney at law. From Edward Markley, counsel, U.S. Radium. One of our expert witnesses has encountered a serious scheduling conflict which makes it impossible for him to testify in April. We have therefore requested an extension until June. As for your request for a settlement— Every case involves some humanitarian aspect. Therefore, I am afraid, that cannot be the basis for settling this one. But I have no doubt you will be rewarded for the good work you are doing. If not in this world, then in the next.

(Cross to:)

SCENE 11

(Grace's home. She sleeps fitfully on a parlor couch.)

GRACE. Mmm. Tommy! Please!

(She sits up with a start to a knocking at the door. The light is refracted, strange, the landscape of dreams. The door swings open and it's MADAME CURIE with a tray of watchdials.)

MADAME CURIE. Rise and shine!

GRACE. Madame Curie?

MADAME CURIE. Time for work!

GRACE. Oh, am I late? I set the alarm.

MADAME CURIE. We have five thousand dials to paint before breakfast. Up, up, up, it's all for the war effort!

GRACE. Please. I'm so very tired.

MADAME CURIE. No complaining! Good soldiers don't complain.

GRACE. But I'm dying.

MADAME CURIE. And who isn't?

(IRENE and KATHRYN appear painting dials.)

IRENE. Get up, Grace!

GRACE. Irene!

KATHRYN. Get up, sleepyhead! You'll never make quota like this.

GRACE. It's not fair! I'm only twenty-six. I should be married by now. I should have children. My own home.

MADAME CURIE. We all have to make sacrifices sometimes.

IRENE. I know I did.

GRACE. But why? Why do we have to make sacrifices?

KATHRYN. It's all for science, Grace.

MADAME CURIE. Science! Family! Every life is sacrificed to something! Just a matter of choosing which.

GRACE. I didn't choose! I didn't have no choice!

KATHRYN. Sure ya did, Grace. *(She licks the brush languidly.)* Sure ya did.

GRACE. Kathryn! Don't do that! *(They all freeze in shock at GRACE's words. Suddenly KATHRYN spits up blood.)* Kathryn?

IRENE. Oh now look what you did, Grace! She's bleeding all over the dials.

GRACE. I'm sorry, Kathryn. I guess I shouldn'ta said anything.

MADAME CURIE *(brightly)*. No problem! What's one more dead dialpainter?

(MADAME CURIE grabs KATHRYN and hustles her out the door with IRENE. Door closes with a bang. Light shift and GRACE is awake in the cold parlor. In the room is a side table, with a basket for the day's mail.)

GRACE. Huh? *(A tapping at the door.)*

MRS. FRYER *(off)*. Grace?

GRACE. Mama.

(Enter MRS. FRYER.)

MRS. FRYER. Grace? Mr. Markley will be here any minute.

GRACE. Mr. Markley?

MRS. FRYER. He's bringing the papers for you to sign. Did you fall asleep?

GRACE. Has Miss Wiley been by?

MRS. FRYER. Miss Wiley?

GRACE. About Kathryn. She told me she might stop by. Did she come by? *(MRS. FRYER turns away, straightening up the room.)*

MRS. FRYER. She might have.

GRACE. Don't you know?

MRS. FRYER. Someone came to the door a while ago—I think your brother answered it. Look, Grace. Ya gotta get ready.

GRACE. They took Kathryn back to the hospital last night—

MRS. FRYER. I know, dear. I know. After ya talk to Mr. Markley, we'll go over there and see how she is. Now, put a comb through that hair.

GRACE. I dreamt she died.

MRS. FRYER. Grace. Don't speak such things.

GRACE. If she dies, it's over.

MRS. FRYER. We're three months behind on the mortgage, Grace.

GRACE. I know that.

MRS. FRYER. Ya can't let this go on.

GRACE. Fifteen hundred dollars—not even a year's wages.

MRS. FRYER. Well, it's better than nothing, ain't it?

GRACE. Is that all I'm worth? Better than nothing?

MRS. FRYER *(stops).* Of course not. Sweetheart. But we got to be realistic. At the rate things are going you'll never get inside that courtroom. And even if ya do—ya can't prove nothin'.

GRACE *(weakly).* Mr. Berry thinks we can.

MRS. FRYER. Mr. Berry ain't payin' the bills. There's the doctor—and the bank. And the coal man. We can't ex-

pect folks to treat us like charity just because you're
sick.

GRACE. Not askin' for charity, Ma. I just want what's
owed to me.

MRS. FRYER. Grace. I know it feels like you're lettin'
Kathryn down. But if she decided to take the company's
offer, would you hold it against her? No. Ya wouldn't.
Now. We'll take that check and pay the bills and whatever is left—you and Tom can have. A little something
to get ya started.

GRACE. There's nothing to start, Ma.

MRS. FRYER. Why do ya have to be so hard on Tommy?

GRACE. Ma. Please don't.

MRS. FRYER. Can't ya see, he just can't face the thought
of ya not bein' with us?

GRACE. I have to face it. Why can't he?

MRS. FRYER. Do something with your hair, Grace. *(She
exits. GRACE gets up with difficulty to prepare for the
meeting. She goes to the mirror to fix herself. Examines
her bandage.)*

GRACE. Two hundred and fifty thousand dollars. What
would you do with two hundred and fifty thousand dollars, Miss Fryer? *(Laughing bitterly.)* Why, I can't imagine. *(Silence.)* No point to it. *(She notices the basket of
mail.)* Ma! You didn't tell me I had mail. *(She takes the
letters out of the basket.)* New Mexico. Huh. They just
keep writing. *(She sorts the letters. GRACE finds a note
in the basket from MISS WILEY.)* She *was* here. Miss
Wiley *was* here! *(Reading the note.)* Ma! Ma! Miss
Wiley was here this morning! She left me a note—

(As GRACE heads to the door, enter MARKLEY and MRS. FRYER.)

MARKLEY. Miss Fryer. Edward Markley. *(He holds out his hand to shake. GRACE doesn't take it. GRACE looks at him, folds her letter away.)*

GRACE. Ma said you brought papers.

MARKLEY. Yes. The terms spelled out as we explained in our letter. Fifteen hundred dollars to you— I've got a check right here. All we need is your signature. *(He gives her the papers. She flips through them.)* It's in triplicate. *(She tries to read, but can't focus.)*

MRS. FRYER. Grace. Mr. Markley is a very busy man.

MARKLEY. Oh, no. Please. Take your time. Look it over carefully. If you prefer, I can leave it and come back tomorrow.

MRS. FRYER. No, no. We'll do this now.

GRACE *(swallows hard)*. What's "hold harmless"?

MARKLEY. You agree to hold the company harmless from any further action.

GRACE. No more lawsuits.

MARKLEY. Correct.

GRACE. Is that just me or anybody in my family?

MARKLEY. Your entire family. It precludes a wrongful-death action also.

GRACE *(looks at the paper again)*. This is a confidential settlement.

MARKLEY. Yes.

GRACE. You didn't say nothin' about it being confidential.

MARKLEY. That's standard for most legal settlements, Miss Fryer. We like to protect our privacy. And your privacy also. It cuts both ways. You agree to keep silent about the terms of the settlement, and so do we.

MRS. FRYER. That seems fair.

MARKLEY. Need a pen? *(MARKLEY takes out a pen, hands it to GRACE. She takes it, looks back at the pages.)*

GRACE. I have another question.

MRS. FRYER. Grace. Mr. Markley already explained the settlement to you.

GRACE. Ma.

MARKLEY. I don't mind.

GRACE. What is contributory negligence, Mr. Markley? *(MARKLEY is puzzled. He looks at the document.)* It's not in that one. It was in them other papers. That you filed. When we did the lawsuit. The radium company said its defense was the statute of limitations and contributory negligence.

MARKLEY. I'm not sure what you're asking, Miss Fryer.

GRACE. It means it's our fault. Don't it?

MARKLEY. It's a standard defense, Miss Fryer. I wouldn't take it personally.

GRACE. How else can I take it?

MRS. FRYER. Mr. Markley. Grace has had an awful headache all day. Maybe you could leave the papers—

GRACE. Maybe he can just answer the question.

MRS. FRYER. Why are you doing this?

GRACE. Why didn't you tell me Miss Wiley was here?

MRS. FRYER. You already made up your mind. She'd only try to talk you out of it.

GRACE. What did she say about Kathryn?

MRS. FRYER. Mr. Markley, if you'll leave the papers, Grace will sign them later.

GRACE. Ma! What did she say about Kathryn?

MRS. FRYER. She said. It don't look good. *(A moment.)*

MARKLEY. Perhaps I should come back later, when Miss Fryer is feeling better.

GRACE. You didn't answer my question, Mr. Markley. And I'd really like an answer. Because, let me tell you: I quit school at fifteen! I went to work at the radium plant because my folks needed the money. At your factory, they told us what to do. When to do it. How to do it. My folks didn't raise me to make trouble. So I didn't make trouble. I did what I was told. I never asked questions! How do you get contributory negligence out of that?

MARKLEY. As I said, it's a standard defense.

GRACE. There's nothin' standard about what happened to me.

MARKLEY. We deeply regret your situation. But there is no evidence to tie your condition to any actions by the U.S. Radium Corporation.

GRACE. Then why are you givin' me this money?

MARKLEY. It's…it's a humanitarian gesture.

GRACE *(laughs)*. A humanitarian gesture?

MRS. FRYER. Mr. Markley. I'll take them papers.

GRACE *(blocking her)*. Humanitarian! Month after month you put us off! Delay after delay. Knowin' how sick we were. How tired. And desperate. Humanitarian! You're waiting for us to die!

MRS. FRYER *(confidentially)*. Grace. Please. Stop this now.

GRACE. Ma. One by one, I watched my friends get sick. And die. In the most horrible way. And you think. I should be grateful? For any spare change they throw at me?

MARKLEY. Miss Fryer. This is a very generous offer, under the circumstances. I would advise you to take it. Because it won't be on the table very long.

MRS. FRYER. What do you mean?

MARKLEY. If Miss Fryer does not sign within twenty-four hours, we will be forced to withdraw our offer. Permanently.

MRS. FRYER. Grace.

GRACE. He's lying.

MARKLEY. I beg your pardon, miss!

GRACE. You're trying to tell me if I don't sign these now—but I came back a week from now and said I changed my mind, you'd still rather go to court? You'd still rather some judge get a look at me...and take your chances I won't win on sympathy alone? Twenty-four hours. You're just trying to bully me.

MARKLEY. Very well, then. Miss Fryer. I'll take that for a no. And we'll see you in court. *(MARKLEY packs up his briefcase and exits as MRS. FRYER sees him out.)*

GRACE. Yes you will! You will see me. If they have to carry me in there, you'll see me. You and Mr. Roeder both!

MRS. FRYER. You call that man back.

GRACE. I'm goin' to court, Ma.

MRS. FRYER. What are you trying to prove? You know you can't win!

GRACE. I want those people to look at me! I want them to look at me and explain how it's my fault I got sick working in their factory!

MRS. FRYER. And what will that get ya? What?

GRACE. Ma. All my life, I've done what other people told me to do. I quit school. Because you said I should. I put that brush in my mouth 'cause Mrs. McNeil said I should. I never said, please can't I finish school? I never said, I don't like the taste of this paint. I never argued. Even though I knew—Ma. I knew somethin' wasn't right. At night, I'd lie in bed, and I'd see my dress. Hanging on the back of the closet door. All aglow. My shoes on the floor. My hairbrush. And comb. On the dresser. So much light, Ma. So much light! And I never once questioned. I never once asked! Don't you see? They knew I wouldn't. *That's* what they were counting on.

(Cross to:)

SCENE 12

(Von Sochocky's home. A knocking off. VON SOCH-OCKY enters to admit ROEDER.)

VON SOCHOCKY. Arthur. So it is you making all this noise.

ROEDER. I left messages with your housekeeper. I know you got the messages. *(A beat.)*

VON SOCHOCKY. As we are no longer in business to-gether, I thought it best not to respond.

ROEDER. Is that what this is about?

VON SOCHOCKY. Perhaps a cup of tea will calm your nerves.

ROEDER. You never told us the paint was dangerous. You never said a word about it—not to me, not to Dan—

VON SOCHOCKY. I didn't know.

ROEDER. You didn't know. You invented the paint, and you didn't know. How can you lie like that?

VON SOCHOCKY. I didn't know until it was too late, Arthur.

ROEDER. I should put you through that wall.

VON SOCHOCKY. Perhaps you should. But you will not. You will sit down. You will have some tea. And you will calm yourself.

ROEDER. I was not the technical man. You were the technical man.

VON SOCHOCKY. Ya. I was the technical man. Sit down, Arthur.

ROEDER. I sold watches, for Christ's sake. I was a salesman.

VON SOCHOCKY. A good one at that. Very good head for the business, you have. Not such a good head for the science, but for the business, very smart. Always you could find ways to cut the costs without losing the quality. That's a gift, Arthur. So. Why don't you have some tea? *(VON SOCHOCKY hands him a teacup. ROEDER sees that VON SOCHOCKY's fingers are black to the second knuckle.)*

ROEDER. Jesus Christ! What's the matter with your hands?

VON SOCHOCKY. It's been that way for some time.

ROEDER. What—have you been—dipping them in ink?

VON SOCHOCKY *(laughs)*. Dipping them in ink? How fond of the pretty story you are. If only it were ink. No. Dr. Martland tells me—it's a necrosis of the tissue. The cells. They are dying. *(ROEDER stares at him.)* With the dialpainters, in the jaw it started. The necrosis. With me, in the hands.

ROEDER. I had no idea.

VON SOCHOCKY. No reason why you should. It's been a long time since I've seen you.

ROEDER. How—how long—

VON SOCHOCKY. But I've known for a while. Miss Wiley—from the Consumer's League—persuaded me to assist Dr. Martland in testing the dialpainters for radium exposure. There aren't that many people around, you know, who can measure that kind of thing. So she came to me. Knowing I had the equipment, and, of course, the skill. I didn't believe her either, Arthur. I didn't want to believe the girls could get sick from working with my paint. I wanted to show her it was a mistake. So I agreed to help. Dr. Martland and I conducted expired air tests on the girls. It was then that I found out. When my own breath registered radioactive. Then my fingers, they began to turn black. *(Beat.)* Now. You wish to have words with me.

ROEDER. I'm sorry.

VON SOCHOCKY. Well. Perhaps now you should make an appointment yourself with Dr. Martland?

ROEDER. Me, what for?

VON SOCHOCKY *(laughs)*. Arthur. You did not notice the glowing dust on your shoes when you went home at night?

ROEDER. How could I miss it? I tracked it all over the house…

VON SOCHOCKY. You can be sure that a good deal of it is now in your lungs. *(VON SOCHOCKY produces the bibliography, tosses it to ROEDER.)* Look familiar?

ROEDER. It's our promotional piece.

VON SOCHOCKY. An excellent promotion. How many new sales did that book account for?

ROEDER. I didn't track it exactly. I like to think it helped our medical market quite a bit.

VON SOCHOCKY. Page ninety-six.

ROEDER. What?

VON SOCHOCKY. Open it. The last chapter. Read it to me?

ROEDER. The last chapter? Radium—Dangerous Effects.

VON SOCHOCKY. Dangerous Effects. How many articles do you have listed there? Ten? Fifteen?

ROEDER. About eighteen, it looks like.

VON SOCHOCKY. How far back do they go, those articles?

ROEDER. I don't know—

VON SOCHOCKY. Look at it. The first one, there. What is the date?

ROEDER. 1906.

VON SOCHOCKY. 1906. Now let me see. When you go into court, you plan to testify that you had no idea radium was dangerous? How do you plan to do that, Arthur? When your own book says that it was. How can you claim that *you* did not know?

ROEDER. I never—I never—really read it.

VON SOCHOCKY. What's that?

(A light shift. As ROEDER talks, the scene around him shifts to the courtroom.)

ROEDER. I never really read it. I hired a man to put it together. I never really...I just glanced at the galleys...I... never read the book.

(*BERRY crosses. ROEDER remains in his chair, which is
now the witness stand. In the courtroom are GRACE and
WILEY, MRS. ROEDER, SOB SISTER, REPORTER,
SOCIETYWOMAN and other members of the public.*)

SCENE 13

BERRY. How do you mean, you never read the book?

ROEDER. It was a standard arrangement. An outside company prepared the piece. They were responsible for the
content.

BERRY. Which you never read.

ROEDER. I think you will find, Mr. Berry, that very few
company presidents read their own promotions word for
word.

BERRY. It has your name on it. You authorized the book's
release. And you had final approval of the content.

ROEDER. Mr. Lee was responsible for our promotional ef-
forts at the time. I entrusted those activities to him.

BERRY. Now, Mr. Roeder. You testified that you started
at the U.S. Radium Corporation in 1918.

ROEDER. Yes, as plant manager.

BERRY. And you held this position for how long?

ROEDER. Four years.

BERRY. During those four years, how often did you venture into the studio?

ROEDER. Every day.

BERRY. Every day. So you must have observed the girls
pointing the brushes on their lips?

ROEDER. I don't recall.

BERRY. You're saying you went into the studio every day and you never saw a single girl put a brush to her mouth?

ROEDER. I said I don't recall it.

BERRY. You don't recall it. What do you recall, Mr. Roeder? You're an awfully young man to have such a faulty memory.

MARKLEY. Objection!

BERRY. I withdraw. No more questions.

COURT. Your witness, Mr. Markley.

MARKLEY. We have no questions for this witness, Your Honor.

COURT. All right, gentlemen. Please approach. I'm ready to issue my ruling.

MARKLEY. Your honor, we have yet to present our defense—

COURT. I realize that, Mr. Markley, but this proceeding is to determine standing. Now, I've heard enough these two days to make that determination. The radium in the bones of these girls is an ongoing source of poison in their systems. Nothing your witnesses can say will change that fact. Will it?

MARKLEY. Our witnesses are prepared to testify that the company could not have known about the danger.

COURT. Mr. Markley, in the interest of justice, I am asking that the defense rest without calling any witnesses. We can conclude this hearing today and schedule the case for trial.

MARKLEY. All right, Your Honor.

COURT. Fine. I therefore rule that the statute of limitations has not been exhausted and these girls have standing to sue.

MARKLEY. Your honor—one thing. I have a very full schedule with two other cases pending, and a key witness will not be available until the end of the summer. We can't be available until September.

BERRY. Your Honor!

MARKLEY. I'm sorry, Your Honor, but our chief expert witness is associated with an institution of higher learning. This is the busiest time of year for him, and I cannot expect him to appear.

BERRY. Mr. Markley is responsible for that situation. He is the one who has demanded continuous delays.

MARKLEY. Your Honor, we've just agreed to waive our right to present witnesses at this hearing. Surely you will not force us to make our defense at trial without the presence of our key witness?

COURT. All right, Mr. Markley. Trial is set for September. This hearing is adjourned.

(COURT disperses. BERRY turns to calm GRACE, and MARKLEY crosses to ROEDER.)

ROEDER. Edward. Why can't Flinn appear?

MARKLEY. He's going to Europe.

ROEDER. Europe? But he's known about this for months. Why would he...oh, very clever, Edward. How long do you plan to keep this up?

MARKLEY. As long as necessary. *(ROEDER realizes that GRACE has gotten up and approached him. He looks away from her.)*

BERRY. Mr. Markley.

MARKLEY. Mr. Berry. Congratulations. I never believed the court would go for it.

BERRY. You know full well these girls can't wait until September. One is so ill she can't appear in court.

MARKLEY. My client has a right to make his defense.

BERRY. We will not wait until September. I promise you that. One way or another—we will find room on the docket—and your expert witness be damned. *(BERRY crosses away to GRACE.)*

ROEDER. That girl is still staring at me.

MARKLEY. I wouldn't worry about it.

ROEDER. She thinks it's personal. That I planned this, somehow. How do I make her understand I didn't want this to happen?

MARKLEY. You don't. You don't make her understand. You don't talk to her.

ROEDER. But she looks like death, Edward.

MARKLEY. They all look like death, Arthur.

(MARKLEY exits, leaving ROEDER. ROEDER realizes that GRACE is still looking at him. MRS. ROEDER crosses to him, takes his arm and leads him out.)

WILEY. Grace?

GRACE. That man, Miss Wiley. He won't look at me. He won't ever look at me. He just looks right past me—like I'm not even here.

WILEY. It doesn't matter, Grace. He heard you.

SCENE 14

(Exit all as SOB SISTER and REPORTER cross forward. During this scene, scene shifts to graveyard.)

SOB SISTER. June 4, 1928! Nancy Jane Harlan for the New York Graphic.

REPORTER. Jack Youngwood for the Ledger!

SOB SISTER. Raymond Berry Seeks Trial Date for Early Summer!

REPORTER. As U.S. Radium Corporation Announces a Settlement!

SOB SISTER. A settlement?

REPORTER. Ten thousand dollars cash for each girl—and twelve dollars a week for life.

SOB SISTER. Twelve dollars a week?

REPORTER. Read all about it in the Ledger. Your first source for news.

(Enter LEE.)

LEE. The company also agrees to pay the medical expenses of each girl for the remainder of her life. And the girls have agreed to submit to a periodic examination by a panel of physicians yet to be appointed. Questions?

SOB SISTER. What led to the settlement?

REPORTER. Is it an admission of responsibility?

SOB SISTER. What about other pending cases?

LEE. It was purely for humanitarian reasons that the U.S. Radium Corporation agreed to the settlement. We admit no liability whatsoever.

SOB SISTER. Where does the company go from here?

LEE. The U.S. Radium Corporation is pleased to have brought this lengthy litigation to a close and looks forward to many more years serving its customers and this community. And that's C.B. Lee—president.

(Enter WILEY.)

WILEY. Katherine Wiley of the New Jersey Consumer's League! Our press statement!

REPORTER. Were you pleased with the outcome, Miss Wiley?

WILEY. Finally these poor girls received some compensation for their suffering. But more importantly the issue of radium poisoning has been brought to public awareness.

REPORTER. Thanks, Miss Wiley.

WILEY. The spelling by the way is Wiley with one "l" and Katherine with a "K." *(WILEY and REPORTER cross off. LEE crosses to MARKLEY.)*

LEE. Well, Edward. It looks like we're back in business.

MARKLEY. What's your game plan?

LEE. Didn't I tell you? I've got a buyer for the tailings that have been piling up behind the building on Alden Street.

MARKLEY. Oh?

LEE. Some contractor in Montclair needs a little infill.

MARKLEY. That's perfect.

(Exit MARKLEY and LEE together. Cross to:)

SCENE 15

(A cemetery. Cool light of an autumn day. GRACE at a gravesite.)

GRACE. Now, Kathryn, this won't do. We can't see your name. *(Clears leaves.)* That's better. Well, Kathryn—I brought my watercolors today. It's such a beautiful day,

too. The trees are starting to turn, but it's still warm—
too warm for a sweater. Not much of a breeze. A fine
day to paint.

*(TOM enters carefully. GRACE sees him but continues
to paint.)*

TOM. Thought I might find you up here.

GRACE. You were right.

TOM. Quiet up here.

GRACE. Yep.

TOM. Well, I guess if you can rest in peace, this is the
place to do it, huh?

GRACE. I guess it is.

TOM *(looks at the painting)*. What do you call that?

GRACE. Watercolors. I'm a little weak when it comes to
landscapes, though.

TOM. No, it's good, Grace. It's nice.

GRACE. First thing I bought with the settlement money
was some paints. Got some oils, too.

TOM. Big spender.

GRACE. Then I bought a car.

TOM. I didn't know you could drive.

GRACE. I can't. My brother's gonna teach me. He drove
me up here today.

TOM. Grace. You wanna learn how to drive, I'd teach you.

GRACE. You got other things to do now, Tommy.

TOM. You know about that.

GRACE. Tommy. Orange just isn't that big.

TOM. I meant to tell you myself, Grace. That's why I
came looking for you—

GRACE. It's all right, Tommy. I'm happy for you. For both of you.

TOM. No hard feelings, then?

GRACE. Oh, Tommy. You think I have time for that?

TOM. I'm glad it worked out for you, Grace. Are you glad? I mean, you don't feel like you backed down too soon, do ya?

GRACE. We didn't back down. They backed down.

(He takes his leave of her as ROEDER enters, much older now, dressed for a much colder day. He sees GRACE and stops. Enter HARRIET, a grown woman now. She is dressed in the style of the 1940s.)

HARRIET. Papa?

ROEDER. It was over here.

HARRIET. Oh, not this again.

ROEDER. This is where I saw her that last time.

HARRIET. This is morbid, Papa.

ROEDER. I stood there for a long time. She didn't notice me at first. But then something made her look up.

GRACE *(looks at him)*. Oh my.

HARRIET. No wonder Mama won't come for drives with you anymore. If this is how you spend your Sundays.

ROEDER. I saw her looking at me. And I looked away.

GRACE. Just like at the courthouse that day. He can't bring himself to look at me.

HARRIET. You need to find another hobby. Retirement isn't good for you.

ROEDER. My heart started pounding, Harriet. I never knew what I would say to her if I had the chance, and suddenly—there she was. And I had the chance.

HARRIET *(lights a cigarette)*. So what did you say?

ROEDER. I couldn't bring myself to speak.

GRACE. It's as if he's *afraid* to look at me. *(She looks back at him, finding strength in that discovery.)*

ROEDER. I had my chance and I couldn't speak.

GRACE. He's afraid of *me*.

HARRIET. Oh, Papa. That was years ago. Why don't you just forget about it? It's not like it was your fault. Nobody knew about things like that, then—science just wasn't as advanced, the way it is now. *(She takes a drag on the cigarette. As ROEDER speaks, lights fade on HARRIET, leaving ROEDER and GRACE alone.)*

ROEDER. I think back on those days—and I try to think—how could it have happened? I remember so clearly climbing the stairs to the studio at Alden Street. At the top of the stairs, those wide, high windows, and the slant of light, the way it hit the floor, the way the floor creaked under my feet—the smell of the place, chalky, like an old schoolroom, and all those girls— schoolgirls, really—all bent to the task, in their plain green smocks, their delicate little hands moving so quickly. No man could work the way those girls did. So careful. So fast. Those brushes flying from the dials to the paint to the dials—to their lips. *(Beat.)* Try as I might, Harriet, try as I might—I cannot remember their faces. *(The irony strikes him.)* I never saw their faces.

(Fade to black.)

END OF PLAY

ACKNOWLEDGMENTS

Radium Girls began nearly six years ago as an idea I pitched to John Pietrowski, artistic director of Playwrights Theatre of New Jersey, in Madison. It was a story that literally took place in John's back yard, and so he immediately said "yes" to my proposal and worked diligently to support what turned out to be a long process of research, writing and revision. My sincere thanks to John and his staff—literary manager Peter Hays, managing director Elizabeth Murphy, publicist Lucy Ann Saltzman and the original Dr. Von Sochocky, Jim Ligon, who doubles in the most essential role of box-office manager. Thanks also to Joseph Megel, who directed the premiere as well as a series of readings and workshops that led up to it. A number of other individuals also assisted me by providing encouragement, opportunity or access to essential information as I researched and developed the script. My thanks to John Eisner of the Lark Theatre; Mark Plesent of The Working Theatre; Chris Smith and J. Holtham of the Ensemble Studio Theatre; Mia McCullough and Brian Russell of The American Theatre Company in Chicago; Lois Densky-Wolff of the Harrison Martland Collection at the University of Medicine and Dentistry of New Jersey; Dr. James Stebbings of Chicago; Dr. Gene Saraceni, now retired from Seton Hill University, Greensburg, Pa.; Shanga Parker at the University of Washington-Seattle; and Tom Donahue, Gail Beach and Grover Gardner at the Catholic University of America and Mace Archer and Lysa Fox of Venture Theatre in Billings, Montana. Particular thanks to Claudia Clark, author of the definitive work on the dialpainters, "Radium Girls: Women and Industrial Health Reform 1910-1935." Claudia personally directed me to materials at the Library of Congress and came to see several productions of the play, offering me a most helpful critique from a historian's perspective—and this during a time when she was battling a life-threatening illness. Her courage and generosity have touched me deeply. And lastly, my love and gratitude to my private cheering section: My husband Paul and my family and friends, particularly Dominique Cieri and Lucy Ann and Simon Saltzman, who housed and fed me during repeated visits to New Jersey to work on the play.

D.W.G.
Silver Spring, Md., April 2003